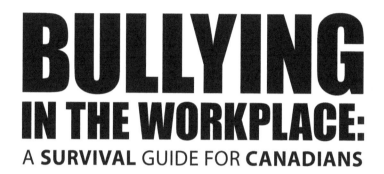

BULLYING
IN THE WORKPLACE:
A **SURVIVAL** GUIDE FOR **CANADIANS**

Dr. Carol Pye

ISBN: 978-1-4834-4925-8 (sc)
ISBN: 978-1-4834-4924-1 (e)

Because of the dynamic nature of the Internet, any web addresses or links contained in this book may have changed since publication and may no longer be valid. The views expressed in this work are solely those of the author and do not necessarily reflect the views of the publisher, and the publisher hereby disclaims any responsibility for them.

Any people depicted in stock imagery provided by Thinkstock are models, and such images are being used for illustrative purposes only.
Certain stock imagery © Thinkstock.

Lulu Publishing Services rev. date: 04/26/2016

CONTENTS

CHAPTER 1

Workplace Bullying an Overview

A Brief Overview of Bullying

There has been an active public discussion about bullying for the last several years. Much of that discussion has been focused on bullying that occurs among school children. Undoubtedly, this focus has been of value in recognizing and addressing the bullying that occurs among children. However, to the observer of the public discussion, it would be too easy to get the impression that bullying stops after children graduate from high school or that bullying among adults is rare and inconsequential. Nothing could be further from the truth. Bullies do not outgrow or end their harmful behaviors when they leave high school. They often get further education, enter the professions, take positions in corporations and work in our public institutions. In those workplace positions, bullies can cause great harm to the people that they target for their destructive behavior. There needs to be a broader public discussion about bullying among adults, most of which occurs in the workplace. Bullying in the workplace is a public health issue that is associated with great mental health harms, great financial cost and lost productivity. We all need to acknowledge the scope of the problem, the harm it causes and the need for a broad based response. Bullying in the workplace is no more a private or individual problem than child abuse is a private family matter.

My perspective on workplace bullying comes from my work as a psychologist. For those of us who provide psychological treatment services, the nature of our work is that we hear many stories of people confronting and surviving painful experiences. The stories of workplace bullying are among the most compelling stories I have heard. There can be little doubt that workplace bullying is prevalent and extremely damaging. A 2012 worldwide survey conducted by Reuters surveyed 14,600 workers in 12 countries. About 30% of them rated their workplace as psychologically unsafe and unhealthy[1]. Similar estimates of prevalence for workplace bullying for US workers show about 30% have been bullied during their working lives[2]. One prevalence estimate for Canada in 2006 was higher: 40% of Canadian workers experienced workplace bullying[3]. People who go through bullying suffer significant psychological impacts and often lose their jobs or even their careers because of the bullying. It can be very challenging to survive workplace bullying. Career RCMP officers have told me that they were more able to cope with threats to their life in the course of their police work than the bullying they later experienced from superior officers. Like most people, the bullying that they experienced from one of their own is not something they could ever have anticipated. The other thing that has impressed me as I worked with people who experienced workplace bullying is that the reality and seriousness of bullying is simply not acknowledged in most organizations. It is scarcely acknowledged by society in general. People who go through workplace bullying are essentially alone in their experience and have few resources to help them deal with it.

For the most part in Canada, it is not illegal to bully someone at work. Employers and organizations usually do not respond well to targets of bullying or offer them any meaningful assistance beyond lip service. Bullying in the workplace needs much greater public recognition and we have a long way to go before we have the type of resources in place to be able to respond adequately to it or reduce is occurrence.

---

[1]   Reuters, 2012

[2]   Workplace Bullying Institute US Surveys: 2010: 35%; 2014: 27

[3]   Lee, The European Journal of Work Organizational Psychology 2006. (V 15:3)

Some Definitions of Workplace Bullying

Workplace Bullying: Canadian Center for Occupational Health and Safety

Bullying usually involves repeated incidents or a pattern of behaviour that is intended to intimidate, offend, degrade or humiliate a particular person or group of people. It has also been described as the assertion of power through aggression... Bullying is usually seen as acts or verbal comments that could 'mentally' hurt or isolate a person in the workplace. Sometimes, bullying can involve negative physical contact as well.

Workplace Bullying: Workplace Bullying Institute, USA, Gary and Ruth Namie

Workplace Bullying is repeated, health-harming mistreatment of one or more persons (the targets) by one or more perpetrators. It is abusive conduct that is :

- Threatening, humiliating, or intimidating, and/or
- Work interference — sabotage — which prevents work from getting done, and/or
- Verbal abuse

These two definitions, one Canadian and one American, have some features in common. They both stress the intentional nature of the bullying. Bullying is not just the actions or statements by someone having an occasional bad day. Both definitions also stress the repeated or chronic nature of bullying behavior. Most people can cope with occasional nasty or rude behavior from co-workers. In contrast, bullying is persistent behaviour and it usually causes harm to its targets. The Workplace Bullying Institute definition stresses that harmful outcomes are an essential component of workplace bullying. In other words, workplace bullying is sufficiently destructive that it would be expected to cause harm to most people.

Differentiating Workplace Bullying from Other Workplace Problems

Some of the terminology used to describe problem behavior at work trivializes the significance of workplace bullying, which is a form of abuse. Workplace bullying is not rudeness, incivility, personality conflict or lack of interpersonal skills. All of these are less severe workplace problems that the majority of workers can deal with adequately; they do not cause serious health outcomes. At the other end of the scale, workplace bullying is not workplace violence. Incidents of physical violence at work are less frequent than bullying[44] and they appear to have different causes and dynamics. Individuals who are from outside of the workplace are responsible for most physically violent and aggressive episodes at work.

1. About 13% of workers experience physical aggression at their workplace. Schat, Frone and Kelloway: Prevalence of Workforce Aggression in the US Workforce in <u>Handbook of Workplace Violence</u>, Kelloway, Barling and Hurrell, 2006, Sage

A Typical Case of Workplace Bullying: A Government Scientist

Note: This case represents some typical workplace bullying experiences and is not based on any actual individual or individuals.

Karen was a new graduate of a science program at a Canadian university. She had excellent credentials and a record of publications in her field of specialization. Karen took a job in a government department where the work has a public safety element. She soon ran into problems with the head of her department who was an older man with less formal qualification than Karen. A few months into her new job, Karen began to have concerns about how scientific data was being treated in public

---

[4]   About 13% of workers experience physical aggression at their workplace. Schat, Frone and Kelloway: Prevalence of Workforce Aggression in the US Workforce in <u>Handbook of Workplace Violence</u>, Kelloway, Barling and Hurrell, 2006, Sage

statements and was particularly concerned about possible public health hazards that could result. Karen raised some of her concerns during a staff meeting. Her boss was clearly displeased by her remarks and soon afterward began a pattern of discriminatory treatment of Karen. The boss required Karen to have her work supervised by a junior, much less qualified, member of staff. He removed a special project from Karen's direction and appointed another member of the staff to direct it, even though he did not have Karen's expertise.

Karen's department had a distinct atmosphere of fear. This surprised her since most of her colleagues were mature professional scientists. She also observed that the colleagues who most consistently supported the department head had significantly preferential treatment from him. Soon, the department head began finding fault with Karen's work in an open and derogatory manner, berating her performance in front of other staff. He began to hold numerous meetings with Karen in which he micromanaged her work. At one point he held a two-hour meeting with her over her request for some routine office supplies. Karen offered to purchase the supplies herself but this did not satisfy him. Throughout the meeting, if Karen looked away to make some notes, he demanded that she look directly at him. The frequent meetings with her boss made it more difficult for her to complete the work that she had been assigned. Karen developed stress symptoms, sleep problems and medical problems: elevated blood pressure and digestive disorders.

Matters escalated for Karen when she got her six-month performance evaluation from her department head. She was rated as unsatisfactory in most categories and described as un-collegial in her dealings with other staff members. As a new graduate with limited experience and as an employee on probationary status, it was apparent to her that bad performance reviews could lead to her termination and difficulty in obtaining a new position. What had been a stressful and unpleasant situation for her now held considerably more threat. Karen consulted the HR office for her department.

After discussing the problems Karen was having with her department head, the HR representative urged Karen to consider mediation with her boss to resolve their "conflict". Karen was very reluctant to take this option as she saw little prospect of its success. She asked to take a couple days to think it over. The day after her conversation with HR,

Karen got a call from the HR manager who wanted to tell her some "good news". Karen's department head had agreed to take a sensitivity training program at the suggestion of the HR manager. After Karen's boss had attended the required two sensitivity training sessions, it became clear to Karen that he was even more angry with her and more determined to take action against her. His criticisms of her work became more personal and nasty. He called her names like "stupid bitch" and made comments to other staff that they should not have to put up with Karen's "incompetence". Also around this time, some upsetting rumors began to circulate via email about Karen's personal life, suggesting that she was a lesbian and that she had serious mental health problems. Karen was hurt and horrified as there was no basis in fact to the rumors. Her coworkers began to avoid her at lunch and coffee time and she felt it was not safe to try to talk to any of the other staff about what was happening to her. After a series of episodes in which the department head misrepresented facts to create documentation of significant problems in Karen's performance; she consulted her union representative and a labour lawyer. The labour lawyer gave Karen some advice but did not offer any hope of a legal remedy, because Karen had union representation. The union representative was sympathetic but did not seem to have much understanding of workplace bullying. She encouraged Karen to document her experiences but told her she would need to maximize her efforts to get on her boss's good side and would need to work harder to demonstrate that she was a diligent employee.

Karen became obsessed with the events at work and constantly talked about them to her fiancé. He was supportive at first but had stresses of his own to deal with. He kept telling Karen to let it go, learn to cope with her difficult boss or look for another job. Karen was not successful in her efforts to let it go when she was with her boyfriend. In time, her stress and preoccupation caused problems between them and he began to withdraw from her.

Karen had a one year probationary period in her job. She struggled to cope with the daily events at work and consulted regularly with her GP, who referred her to a psychologist to help her manage her stress. Karen found the counseling helpful but her health and her relationship continued to suffer.

Karen got another very negative performance evaluation toward the end of her probationary period and consulted with the union representative again. When she arrived for work the next morning, her boss met her accompanied by a security guard. The boss handed Karen a termination letter and advised her that she had to leave the building. She was allowed one hour under security supervision to pack up her personal belongings. Then she was escorted out of the building, with her shocked colleagues watching.

Karen had a month of severance pay and had to take Unemployment Insurance while she hunted for another job. She had no letters of reference, so it proved to be challenging. Using her university contacts, she was able to find a position ten months later. However, the new job involved a move to another province, far away from her hometown. The new job represented a major career setback. Karen's career did not fully recover from its bad start. Her relationship with her fiancé ended and she had financial problems. Her health continued to suffer and she was plagued by psychological symptoms for a few years. She continued with therapy and eventually went back to university to retrain for a different type of work.

A number of years later, Karen ran into her old university supervisor at a social event. He asked what had happened to her. She gave him a brief version and he replied, "Karen, this is such a loss; our field has lost one of the most promising young scientists who trained under my supervision".

A Typical Time Course of Workplace Bullying

Bullying tends to show a pattern of escalation over time. By its nature, workplace bullying usually involves persistent, repetitive behavior by one or more workplace figures toward an individual targeted employee. At first, the targeted person will probably have trouble making sense of the behavior of the bully or will try to find a reasonable explanation for the bully's actions. The target will often make efforts to improve things with the bully by working harder or trying to "communicate" more effectively with the bully. Such efforts by the target rarely lead to any improvement. It is only with repeated bad experiences that the target will come to realize that they are being singled out for unfair treatment for reasons that defy understanding . Subjectively, it often feels like being singled out for undeserved hatred and that is a deeply disturbing experience for most people.

Workplace observers of the interactions will typically give the benefit of the doubt to the bully, who usually holds a higher position. The majority of observers will engage in some victim blaming. Nasty rumors may circulate about the target. Typically the sorts of rumors that circulate have unpleasant or prejudicial content about the target, such as allegations about sexual conduct, substance abuse or mental health problems. It can be difficult or impossible to address rumors of a personal nature that circulate in a work environment but rumors can be very damaging. The target tends to become more isolated from the work group and generally does not have support or assistance from workmates. Unfortunately, efforts by the target of bullying to seek assistance from upper management, human resources or union personnel usually have disappointing results. Many organizations will have reasonable formal harassment policies in place but they seldom have adequate evaluation procedures and the favored intervention strategies are generally ineffective. Upper management and human resources staff may be biased toward bullies who hold power in the organization. Union personnel may be uninformed about the nature of bullying and may not have any real power to deal with it, if they are able to identify it. Bullies in the workplace may have a number of complaints against them, say from serial targets. Management personnel faced with such charges of bullying may offer a variety of interventions like sensitivity training or anger management that will usually have little benefit.

Mediation and training courses are not appropriate or effective in most cases of bullying. Mediation works best when parties of similar rank or power are involved and that is seldom the case with bullying. Bullying in the workplace is improperly understood if it is defined as a "personality conflict". Similarly, most bullying does not seem to arise from deficits in skills that can be readily addressed through classroom training. Sensitivity training and anger management would have little or no beneficial effect on the behavior of most bullies.

Generally, the bully sees nothing wrong with their own behavior and in fact, has a lifetime history of being rewarded for that behavior, advancing over others and frequently getting the results they want through bullying.

One of the consequences of bullying in a work environment is that other workers may perceive that their own interests in the workplace could be compromised by openly supporting the target or taking a sympathetic position toward the target.

Most people will say as little as possible and will try to remain "neutral". Their neutrality can serve to strengthen the bully's efforts. It can be especially hurtful to a target if they confided in someone at work, only to have that person later pull away from them. Feeling increasingly isolated at work, and being discouraged by the failures of authorities to understand or intervene; the target will typically engage in a battle for survival. They try to buffer or block the worst of the bully's damage and try to hold on to their job and reputation. Such battles can be prolonged and they often fail in their objectives. Loved ones may urge the target to just quit their job but that is rarely a realistic option or one that the target would accept. The battle for survival can last months or years. As time passes, there is an increasing toll on the health, emotional reserves and productivity of the target, in spite of their best efforts. It is not unusual for the target to be affected to such an extent that they need a leave of absence from work, which can further compromise the security of their employment. In a large percent of bullying cases, the target is fired or forced to quit the job they fought so hard to keep. Recovery from the experience of workplace bullying can be lengthy and challenging.

CHAPTER 2

The Factors that Contribute to Bullying

When bullying becomes a problem in a work environment, there are apt to be several different contributing factors.

The most likely situation for bullying to occur is one in which two main factors come together:

- A problem personality who holds power or authority in the workplace: the bully
- Someone who, in some way, is seen as a threat by the problem personality: the target

Workplace bullying is not a problem that can be adequately understood by focusing only on certain types of "victims". Popular opinion holds the view that bullying victims must be lacking in some skills or attributes; they must be people who do not know how to cope or do not understand how to "play the game" at work. Casual observers and even professionals, such as HR directors, labour lawyers or union representatives; often focus on the targets of bullying with a view to finding out how they invited or caused their own mistreatment This "blame the victim" attitude is comparable to the attitudes toward women who have been physically abused in an intimate relationship. The naïve observer thinks "They must be doing something wrong to be treated this way". However, like the batterer, the workplace bully is the one who has the problem. Just like domestic abusers, bullies are apt to have several victims or a series of targets over time. Well functioning and capable people can become the target of bullying in the workplace.

Work place bullying among adults has some similarities to bullying among children but there are significant differences. Children are apt to bully a child who is smaller, younger, weaker, odd or vulnerable in some way. Adult bullies are more apt to target someone who represents a threat to the power they hold or seek.

Research suggests that targets of bullying tend to be particularly valuable employees: experienced, knowledgeable, ethical, principled and collaborative. It is these very positive qualities that represent some manner of psychological threat to a certain kind of insecure or uneasy power holder. The bully believes "This person could make me look bad" or "She may know more than I do about the work we are doing here."

Environmental or organizational factors can contribute to the prevalence of bullying. A corporate culture that rewards profits or results, regardless of the cost, and fails to hold power players accountable for their behavior will result in higher rates of workplace bullying. Rewarding interpersonal aggressiveness can create a climate in which bullies thrive. An organization with a culture that devalues empathy and accountability will also likely have higher rates of bullying.

Some groups of workers appear to be at higher risk to become targets of bullying, particularly those of a minority or devalued group status. Gender and racial biases appear to play a role, as women and blacks report higher rates of workplace bullying experiences.

We live in a culture that holds some cherished beliefs about work achievement and economic success.[5] There are deeply held beliefs that people advance in the workplace on the basis of their personal merit and effort. North Americans and many Europeans typically believe in a meritocracy. In this way of thinking, if someone has advanced to a position of authority in an organization, they are seen as deserving of that position. This creates a significant bias in favor of anyone who holds power and gives bullies who hold formal power credibility and advantages that are not granted to their targets.

Group dynamics come into play in the work place environment in a manner that can magnify the effectiveness of the bully. Other employees who observe some of the bullying, but are not directly engaged in it, will generally support the bully and will not provide assistance to the

---

[5] R H Tawney, Religion and the Rise of Capitalism. 1926

target of bullying. It is not completely clear why this should be the case but there are plausible reasons why observers give the advantage to the bully. People like to align with power holders, they prefer to be on the winning side and do not want to become targets of the bully themselves. Self interest will tend to line up other workplace players in support of the bully. Usually the target of bullying becomes very isolated in the work environment. It is extremely rare for any other person to confront a bully at work, especially a bully who holds significant power. Unfortunately, it is also rare that senior authorities in an organization will deal effectively with the bully.

Who Engages in Bullying

There is not enough research information to answer this question confidently but there are some indications in the research and literature about workplace bullying. There is a distinct association between holding organizational power and being a bully. Some research shows that a majority of bullies are in positions of authority in the work place.[6] These bullies abuse the authority they hold in the organization. It is the very power they hold that they use to bully their targets. A typical tactic of the abuse of authority bully is the use of the performance appraisal. Often the performance appraisal is used to misrepresent the target's functioning or even to prepare the path to have the target demoted, sidelined or fired. A significant percentage of people who have experienced chronic bullying lose their jobs either by being fired or by becoming disabled from the effects of the bullying. Some estimates suggest that 75% of bullying targets are fired or forced to quit their jobs.

It appears likely that many bullies have specific kinds of personality problems. Aggression is a human trait that is distributed like other traits such as height or intelligence, along a bell curve More aggressive individuals are more motivated to seek power and may be more apt to abuse it when they hold it. Similarly, the capacity to feel empathy for others varies along a continuum. People with significant deficits in empathy for others will feel no discomfort about causing harm to their

---

[6]   WBI National Survey 2010: 81 % of bullies are in positions of authority

subordinates or workmates and they may even take pride in their ability to exploit, gain advantage or prevail over others.

Some personality types are probably more prevalent among bullies, especially those with deficits in empathy or aggressive tendencies. Narcissists and psychopaths have personality styles that are attracted to power holding. They will strive to rise through the organizational structure to the highest possible levels. Some research indicates that there are higher rates of psychopaths, for example, in the top ranks of corporations than in prison populations. It is the failed or less adept psychopaths who get into legal difficulty and eventually are incarcerated. The successful ones are running organizations. They are often well regarded due to their powers of deception and their convincing favorable self-presentation. Machiavellian behavior in organizations is often remarkably successful. Machiavellian personalities appear to spend a great deal of their time at work, plotting and scheming how to promote their own advancement and personal benefit. They can be particularly adept at influencing other people and seem to quickly learn the motivations and weaknesses of those around them.

Who Gets Bullied

One intriguing finding from bullying research is that the profile of a typical target of workplace bullying is the same profile as that of a very valuable employee. The profile of a typical target shows an employee who is experienced, knowledgeable, capable, well motivated, cooperative with co-workers and well liked by others. Targets of bullying tend to have strong personal principles and will act on principle ahead of their own immediate interests. This characteristic would suggest that it would not be easy for an unprincipled boss to control or manipulate them. A worker could become a threat to a workplace power holder by speaking out against some type of wrongdoing such as improper or harmful organizational practices. The bully might then retaliate or begin a campaign to remove the target from their job.

A typical scenario is one in which a boss with a personality problem has a particularly capable and experienced employee working for them. The boss may be less experienced, less capable or less confident in their own abilities than the employee. Sometimes the problem boss is new to their supervising role and wants to establish their dominance. The capable employee seems to represent some manner of threat to the self-image of the problem boss. Interactions between them soon evolve into bullying by the problem boss, even when the employee is just doing their job in their usual and entirely satisfactory manner.

Sometimes an individual who has not been bullied previously in their workplace will be bullied during a time of vulnerability, such as following the death of a loved one or after returning to the workplace after treatment for cancer. A bully lacking in empathy may become angry or impatient with the limitations the individual shows in their work performance during such a vulnerable time. The bully will start pressuring or harassing the vulnerable individual in an effort to increase their performance to their previous level. Of course, this only makes things worse for someone who is struggling to do their best under difficult circumstances.

Sexism and Racism as Factors in Bullying

Research on bullying shows that women and racial minorities experience higher rates of workplace bullying than the general population. It is likely that persons with disabilities and sexual minorities are also more apt to be targeted by workplace bullies. We do not know enough about bullies to be sure of their motivations, but it does seem that there is some overlap between bullying and other forms of mistreatment based on discrimination. In a sense, both racism and sexism are forms of bullying, with specific visible target groups. There is an affinity between bullying and power motivation. Bullies may see themselves as entitled to positions of advantage over others. They may like to exercise power over people who they believe are not their equals. Racists and sexists have false beliefs in the superiority of their own group. When they encounter someone who challenges these false beliefs, such as a highly intelligent black person or a strong capable woman, they may feel threatened and then attempt to assert their presumed superiority.

Some Special Types of Bullying

Abuse of Authority

As noted earlier, many bullies hold formal power over the targeted employee. When the bully misuses the power they hold in their workplace, they are engaging in Abuse of Authority. Some typical examples of this sort of bullying are when the bully supervisor inappropriately takes work away from the target that he or she has been performing well. Often this would be a valued project or something the target takes pride in doing well. It heightens the impact if the bully then assigns the valued work project to someone considerably less qualified to complete the work. Constantly changing work requirements in a manner that becomes harassing is another form of abusing authority. Similarly, assigning an overload of work responsibilities can become abusive. There are a variety of other methods that belong in this category: denials of training opportunities, denial of necessary leave, pressure to take on unpaid overtime, adding nuisance tasks to the workload, and other manipulations of daily work life that can be seen as forms of managing. In reality, these methods are forms of mismanagement that harm both the target and the work that is supposed to be performed under the bully's supervision. The bully will set the target up to fail, then he will use the evidence of that failure against the target. A favorite tool of Abuse of Authority bullies is to create a file on the employee that can be used to discipline or fire them. The performance review is a tool that is often abused by Abuse of Authority bullies. Most evaluation forms leave plenty of room to make negative comments about workers that can be hard to verify or challenge. A bully boss will use this method of discrediting an employee that he is hoping to be able to dismiss. A paper trail is constructed against the employee, then that invented documentation is used to justify the dismissal of the target.

Unquestionably, the behavior of Abuse of Authority bullies can be both costly and damaging to an organization but it can be hard to prove that their actions constitute abuse. If the abuse meets a certain legal test, the target may have a case for constructive dismissal. For example, a worker is hired to perform a job for which he is well qualified and after a few months on the job, he becomes the target of a boss who is a bully who has never been called to account by anyone in authority over him. The bully may then change the job requirements for the target such that the job is no longer the one he was hired to do and the new role may be one that is quite unsuitable for him. In such a case, it would be best for the target to consult a lawyer to see if he has a case against the company, which is ultimately responsible for the bully's conduct in carrying out the duties of his position. Targets of Abuse of Authority bullies need to be vigilant to keep their own set of accurate records to be able to counter the claims of the bully boss.

Whistleblowers

The worker who is prepared to speak out about some form of wrongdoing in their organization represents an acute threat to those engaged in the wrongdoing or benefiting from it. Those who are complicit or operating by expediency in such a compromised situation will view the whistleblower as unpredictable and uncontrollable. The whistleblower is putting his own notion of right and wrong ahead of the norms prevailing in his workplace. Efforts to eliminate the whistle-blower from the workplace or to exact revenge on her can be extreme in many of these cases. There are few resources to protect whistle blowers who often pay a very high price for trying to do the right thing.

What Happens to the Whistleblowers

RCMP Case

RCMP Corporal Catherine Galliford became a familiar face on Canadian television as the spokesperson for the Air India Bombing investigation and the Missing Women's Task Force during the Robert Picton murder investigation in BC. She spurred an investigation into sexual assault, harassment and misconduct within the RCMP after she filed a detailed 115-page internal complaint in 2011. Among other things, she alleged that RCMP officers working on the missing women case watched porn and skipped work instead of working on the missing women's case. She detailed chronic sexual harassment from senior officers. Galliford said after 16 years of service, she had reached a breaking point. She also said she was diagnosed with post-traumatic stress disorder and other disorders. Galliford's complaint served as a catalyst, prompting other female officers to come forward with similar complaints of long term sexual harassment by fellow officers in the Force.

RCMP Case

By February 2016, there were 440 women RCMP members who are potential claimants for a planned class action lawsuit against the Force. Many of the claimants were veteran officers with many years of service in the RCMP. They represent all ten Canadian provinces. The claimants are waiting to have their case certified for a class action. Cpl Galliford launched her own lawsuit against the RCMP in 2012, which is scheduled to come to trial in 2016. The RCMP denied her allegations in a publicly released statement in 2012. In their public statements, they portrayed Cpl Galliford as an alcoholic who had refused treatment a number of times. Presumably the effort to publicly discredit Cpl Galliford and her accusations took priority over any regard to protect confidential health information for a member of the Force. The RCMP took steps to dismiss Cpl Galliford from the Force in 2013, notifying her of their intent to discharge her.

In 2014 the Canadian government passed new legislation, Bill C-42, allowing the RCMP powers to dismiss problem members, the so-called "bad apples". Many people familiar with the way the RCMP operates in personnel matters are concerned that the Force will use its new powers to dismiss whistleblowers and members who are struggling with PTSD. (See MacLeans Feb 27, 2015)

Health Canada Scientists

Health Canada scientists Dr Shiv Chopra, Dr Margaret Haydon and Dr Gerard Lambert had been raising concerns since the 1990s, claiming their bosses at the Veterinary Drugs Directorate had been pressuring them to approve drugs that could pose health hazards. One particular drug was a Montsano drug, rBST, a bovine growth hormone.

The Senate held an inquiry about this drug and the three scientists raised their concerns during testimony before the Senate committee. Eventually the Senate decided it would not approve the drug. However, the matter received considerable press coverage. There were several more incidents in which the three scientists went public with their concerns about the department policy at their workplace, the Veterinary Drug Directorate. All three were fired in 2004 for insubordination and from that time they began fighting to get their jobs back.

The Public Service Labour Relations Board considered their cases and ruled in 2011 that Lambert was dismissed unfairly and should be reinstated, however they ruled that Chopra or Haydon were not unfairly dismissed; they were not reinstated. It did not enhance the optics of the decision that Lambert was the one white male in the group of three scientists. Based on a technicality, the decision to reinstate one scientist and not his two colleagues caused concern for the Professional Institute of the Public Service of Canada. All three scientists had put the public interest ahead of their own interests. The Labour Board ruling was seen as a setback for whistle blowing in Canada. (CBC: The Fifth Estate, October 19, 2012)

A Teacher Who Spoke Out About Child Sexual Abusers Being Reinstated by the Ontario College of Teachers.

Jim Black is an Ontario Teacher who retired with 30 years of teaching experience and a strong reputation among his peers. He was nominated for the Prime Minister's Award for Teaching Excellence in 2002 and served on the Ontario College of Teachers' Council from 2002 to 2003. The Ontario Ministry of Education asked him to provide an evaluation of the Ontario College of Teachers and he produced a report that was critical of the College for allowing sexual offenders back into the classroom. He recommended a number of significant changes to College policies. Following his report, he experienced a series of reprisals. He retired in 2006 and got some media attention for making his report public. The College then began disciplinary action against him for vague offences. Although he was retired, he was threatened with fines and suspensions. In 2009, he was suspended from teaching for 24 months and fined $ 1000. Allegedly, by 2012, no reforms were made by the Ontario College of Teachers to address the problems that Mr Black had identified; specifically, sexual offenders were getting their teaching licenses reinstated by the College. (Canadians for Accountability, Ian Bron Feb 7, 2012) (CBC Marketplace, April 7, 2016: Burying Teachers' Bad Behavior)

Whistleblower Protection Legislation in Canada Public Servants Disclosure Protection Act 2011

The Canadian Government passed the Public Servants Disclosure Protection Act in 2007. It applies to most of the federal public sector employees; government departments, crown corporations, the RCMP and other federal public sector bodies. Under the Act, the Office of the Public Sector Integrity Commissioner, PSIC, provides a confidential method for public sector employees to report wrongdoing in the public sector. However the Commissioner has the option of not investigating a report made to PSIC. The Act also established a Public Servants Disclosure Protection Tribunal (PSDPT), which can hear complaints of reprisals against whistleblowers.

Under the Public Servants Disclosure Protection Act, whenever a finding of wrongdoing is upheld by an investigation conducted by the PSIC office, it must be reported to Parliament and the Senate. In the years following the proclamation of the Act, there were only nine reports to Parliament. In contrast, the Federal Accountability Initiative for Reform reports about 100 calls from whistleblowers each year. The PSDPA legislation has been called an "expensive exercise in futility", with 40 million dollars in costs and almost nothing to show by way of results[7]. The first PSIC Commissioner made no findings of wrongdoing in three years and she resigned in the wake of a damning report by Auditor General, Sheila Fraser. The PSDPT has never made a finding in favor of a whistleblower claiming reprisals.

In Canada, whistleblowers can expect to be suspended without pay. It is easy to harass and fire a whistleblower in most organizations.

---

[7] David Hutton, FAIR, Dec 20 2013

Typically the whistleblower will find that avenues of redress are blocked to them. Grievances are rarely successful, as they are under the control of people with authority in the organization. Typically, these are the very people who are at the center of the whistleblower's complaints. Canada has lagged behind other countries in terms of whistleblower protection. In recent years, there have been repeated calls for more effective legal protection for whistleblowers in all sectors of the Canadian economy, both public and private.[8]

Career Assassination

One of the most extreme forms of workplace bullying is Career Assassination. While a lot of bullying seems to be designed to make the target diminished, easily controlled and miserable; Career Assassination goes much further. The objective of this form of bullying appears to be complete destruction of the reputation and career prospects of the target. A typical bully might be satisfied by firing his target from her job in the organization, usually after a few years of bullying and the creation of a personnel file to justify the dismissal. The career assassin, however, would not be satisfied with simply firing his target, the assassin would want to destroy the target's professional reputation to the point that the target could no longer work in his field of expertise. Such extreme forms of bullying may be more apt to occur among elite or highly specialized groups such as academics, scientists or medical specialists. In cases of Career Assassination, the stakes are very high. The target must fight to protect not just his job and income but his very professional identity and a lifetime career investment that cannot be replaced. A number of factors can increase the impact of high stakes bullying of this sort. Where a target works in such a specialized field of expertise that there are a small number of job opportunities for them, they are rendered more vulnerable. A medical specialist who is working in one of only three highly specialized hospital departments in the English speaking world cannot easily relocate or hunt for another job if they become the target of a high status bully in their department. Both the target and

---

8   Ian Bron, Dec 9, 2013 Transparency International Canada for the UN Convention on Corruption

the bully would be well aware of the difficulty the target would face if he wanted to find another position

The other factor that can increase the stakes would be the personality characteristics of the assassin. If the assassin has the traits of psychopathy, the bullying will assume more extreme forms. Psychopaths can and do enter the professions and it is not unusual for them to be attracted to positions of power and influence. They lack empathy and conscience and are often skillful in influencing others. Such a person who targets a subordinate or colleague would take any measures that would suit their purpose. For example, they might take credit for the research or writing of the target or they might steal intellectual property such as an invention. They would be capable of spreading lies and rumors about the target, falsifying documents and making damaging accusations, for example, about mental health problems or disturbing sexual behavior by the target. Even when unproven, such accusations or rumors can do considerable harm.

Career Assassination will typically have more damaging effects on the target and it will be harder to fight to protect the target's job and career prospects. Evidence collection is even more important in this type of bullying and could include such measures as legally permitted audio recordings. Anyone who suspects that they are being targeted for a career assassination would be well advised to develop a poker face, to reveal as little as possible about personal matters and to carefully guard their work, files and documents. Unfortunately, psychopathic assassins are typically good at creating allies and spies. The target may be a friendly and trusting person normally, but in this situation, they would need to exercise great caution about confiding in anyone connected to the workplace. Finding safe, confidential and expert advice would be particularly important to survive a career assassination effort.

In extreme circumstances, the battle for survival carries its own distinct psychological risks. How does a person survive a battle with an unscrupulous adversary without resorting to the kind of tactics that person uses to do you harm? It is no small challenge. For psychological survival however, fighting for your survival in a way that is true to who you are is the best way to ensure a long range favorable outcome. For a person of integrity, it will harm them psychologically if they become like the harmful person by assuming their tactics. Sometimes the target's career, as it existed, will not survive the assassination. The person may still find a way to survive and rebuild their life. Several years ago, I heard an account of a high profile, highly qualified expert who ran into difficulty with some powerful people in his field. He had to give up the career in which he had excelled and for which he had many years of training. He dropped off my radar for several years. Then I learned that he was working in a skilled trade and was enjoying a simpler life, free of the professional politics that had brought his career to an end.

CHAPTER 3

The Effects of Bullying

The Effects of Bullying on Targets and on the Workplace

Most people can cope with a fair bit of interpersonal unpleasantness without suffering significant harm to their health. However, workplace bullying needs to be distinguished from less stressful forms of ordinary bad behavior among individuals in the work environment, such as "incivility". Just as bullying is distinguished by its personalized, intentional, repetitive and sustained nature, its consequences are much more serious than the consequences of more ordinary forms of bad behavior. Harmful consequences of bullying affect the targeted worker, the workplace observers, overall productivity in the wokplace and the financial health of the organization. When bullying is allowed to prevail in an organization, the climate of the workplace will become unhealthy and degraded.

The most obvious effects of bullying are on the targeted individual. People who have been bullied regularly at work generally develop psychological symptoms and can show a syndrome that is very similar to Post Traumatic Stress Disorder. Often, they experience intense distress and respond with strong emotions and physiological overreaction to key events in their workplace. Health problems may be associated with the physiological overreaction, such as gastric problems or high blood pressure. Poor concentration, irritability and sleep problems are common. The targeted person may become very anxious, preoccupied with their problems at work and may suffer mood disturbances. They are unable to relax and have fun, even if that is their normal personality. They may show avoidance or withdraw from their usual activities and enjoyments. They might block out some of the upsetting events or have trouble remembering important aspects of what has happened to them. Hypervigilant and unable to think of little else but their battle to survive at work, they can seem completely obsessed with their work situation.

Spouses complain that targets talk about the work situation and the bullying constantly and have lost the ability to enjoy their personal relationships. Normal positive feelings may be restricted. Relationships and work performance can suffer, particularly if the bullying lasts for many months or years. The sense of a future is darkened for the individual and they can see no good future for themselves. The longer the bullying lasts and the more severe it is, the more likely the individual will suffer the above mentioned types of effects in their psychological health and various medical problems linked to stress.

There is reason to believe that the harmful effects of bullying extend to observers as well as the person directly targeted. Bullying that is obvious to others in the work environment can create a climate of fear that could have a negative effect on everyone in the work environment. Bullying that is unchecked or even rewarded by upper management also undermines the confidence and respect that the workers would otherwise have in their organization.

As the work climate is degraded by ongoing bullying, a range of negative effects could be anticipated, such as increased use of sick time. Some research suggests that work performance declines after an episode of bullying, not just for the targeted individual, but for all workers who observed the bullying event, so there would be economic consequences for any organization that does not actively control and eliminate bullying.

Can Bullying Result in Post Traumatic Stress Disorder

This question does not have a simple answer. According to the diagnostic manual used by mental health professionals, the DSM V, Post Traumatic Stress Disorder can only be diagnosed in people who have experienced certain types of traumatic events that involved risk to life of self or others, risk of bodily harm or sexual assault. While such events do happen in the workplace, they are rare and most bullying does not involve life threatening events or risk of bodily harm. However, many mental health professionals who treat people who have been severely bullied at work have noted that these individuals develop a set of symptoms that are the same as those shown by people with PTSD.

The question has been receiving more research attention. An interesting comparison is with domestic abuse. Researchers who have studied the rate of PTSD in victims of domestic abuse have found that PTSD symptoms are more strongly associated with psychological abuse than with physical abuse[9]. This suggests that deliberate infliction of psychological harm needs to be more adequately reflected in the diagnostic system. Researchers who have been investigating symptoms of PTSD in people bullied at work have found rates as high as 42% of targets meeting all of the PTSD diagnostic criteria, except for having experienced a life threatening or physically harmful event[10].

It can be argued that the diagnostic system is a work in progress and it may eventually recognize that some cases of PTSD develop without the prior occurrence of a life-threatening event. Members of the RCMP who have experienced both life threatening events and severe bullying by a superior officer, often report that the bullying was more harmful to their mental health than the occupational hazard of a serious physical threat. We know that traumatic events that have an element of human error or human malice are more likely to result in significant PTSD than naturally occurring disasters. This suggests that experiencing severe harm from someone deliberately damaging your professional identity and ability to make a living would be a particular risk for psychologically harmful outcomes. To put this in some perspective, a majority of people who undergo serious bullying at work do actually lose their jobs eventually, either by being fired or by being unable to continue work due to the severe consequences of bullying on their health.

---

[9]   Arias & Pape, Violence and Victims, 14, 55-67, 1999
[10] Rodriguez-Munoz et al, Journal of Applied Psychology, 2010, v 40 10 2616-2635

What is the Financial Cost of Bullying?

Some of the information about the financial cost of bullying in the workplace is buried in the statistics on the financial cost of stress and mental health problems in the workplace. Both of these more generic terms would include some of the consequences of workplace bullying, the percentage being unknown. The data on cost of workplace stress or mental health problems does not allow any calculation of the subset of problems and costs specifically caused by or related to work place bullying. Most estimates of stress in the workplace show significant levels of worker stress. For example, a ten month survey, Your Life at Work, 2014, conducted for the Globe and Mail by Globe Careers and Howatt HR Consulting included 7,300 respondents to the survey. Sixty percent of the respondents reported feeling stressed and unable to manage the pressures of their work and private life. Stressed respondents also typically reported that they did not have strong coping skills to manage the stress they were experiencing. Employees in the most stressed group indicated that their employers were too demanding and they did not have the tools to do their jobs adequately. While the survey report emphasized the need for workers to improve their stress coping skills, it did not attempt to analyze or discuss the impact of workplace conditions as a major contributor to worker stress levels.

Looking at the costs of mental health issues, the Life and Economic Impact of Major Mental Illnesses in Canada 2011 to 2041 done by Risk Analytica for the Mental Health Commission of Canada estimates an annual cost to business of $ 6 Billion per year in costs to business from employee mental health problems. This figure includes absenteeism and lost productivity while at work and does not include such costs as EAP programs or disability leave costs. The private sector spends between $180 and $300 million a year on short-term disability costs and an additional $ 135 million on long-term disability costs[11].

We need to do a better job of acknowledging how the workplace itself generates a proportion of these mental health consequences. While mental health problems are complex and influenced by many factors, negative events play a significant role in precipitating or causing many

---

[11]   Lopez Pacheo, Financial Post, February 2013.

psychological problems. Where workplace factors are contributing to mental health problems, employers have both the power and the responsibility to address those causes of stress. Bullying is among the most severe form of stress that the workplace can inflict upon a worker. Bullying is not an uncommon or trivial work place problem, so the financial cost of it is likely to be significant. Some evidence suggests that bullying is widespread, with prevalence estimates of 30%, or more, of employees reporting experiences of having been bullied at work. There are a variety of costs that are associated with bullying. These would include increased sick time, short and long term disability leave, reduced productivity in the workplace, replacement costs for workers who leave an organization after being bullied and legal costs for bullying related lawsuits against organizations.

It can be difficult to get a reliable estimate of the financial cost of bullying but there are studies that attempt to address the question. One of the most basic costs from workplace bullying is increased sick days for workers who are being bullied. Scandinavian researchers have shown that bullied employees have considerably more sick time, about 25 % more than non-bullied workers[12]. Workdays lost due to bullying alone in the UK are estimated at about 19 million a year according to figures provided by Royal Sun Alliance, a UK insurance company. They also estimate that at this rate, lost workdays cut into company profits by as much as 10 percent.

Bullying also reduces productivity. Bill Sutton of Stanford University has estimated that productivity in a workplace where bullying prevails could decline by as much as 40%. Some Canadian data is consistent with this. The Canada Safety Council estimates that organizations that manage their employees well will outperform those that do not manage employees well by 30 to 40%[13].

Employees are lost to organizations through bullying. US figures from the Workplace Bullying Institute suggest that about 70% of bullied employees will leave their jobs after an average of 6.7 years of employment[14]. There would be considerable replacement and training

---

[12]   Kivimaki et all Workplace bullying and sickness absence in hospital staff, Occupational Environmental Medicine 2000 Oct 57 (10) 656-60
[13]   Canadian Safety Council: Bullying in the Workplace, 2000
[14]   Namie, Workplace Bullying Institute 2003

costs from this rate of turnover. Rayner and Keashly estimated a total of 1.2 million dollars, US, for an organization of 1000 employees for the replacement cost of workers who leave as a result of being bullied or affected by bullying in their environment[15]. In the UK; Hoel, Sparks and Cooper analyzed the costs from bullying and estimated a cost of 1.88 billion pounds a year, plus the cost of lost productivity[16].

In addition to sick days, productivity decreases, and increased employee turnover, there are other costs associated with workplace bullying: increased short and long term disability claims, and the potential for legal costs from employees who have wrongful dismissal or constructive dismissal suits against the organization. Legal action against an organization can be very costly, particularly if successful.

One promising development in the area of determining the financial cost of bullying is a calculator developed by Dr Dan Dana. His Dana Measure of Financial Cost of Conflict, 2014 allows an organization to make a determination about the probable cost of conflict and bullying in their specific workplace. Data about financial costs to employers is likely to be particularly important in advocacy efforts to get employers to become more effective in addressing bullying.

[15]   Rayner and Keashly, Bullying at Work, APA, 2005
[16]   Hoel Sparks and Cooper, 2001, The Cost of Violence/Stress at Work. eScholarID:5b464

CHAPTER 4

Bullying in Particular Occupations

A number of authors have suggested that particular occupational groups have higher than average rates of bullying. This can be difficult to determine with any certainty, given the differences in definitions and study methods. However, there are some relevant findings on this question and some of the data is Canadian.

Armed Forces

The Armed Forces in the UK have reported recent increases in rates of bullying in military settings. According to a 2014 survey, one in ten military personnel claimed to be the victim of discrimination, harassment or bullying in an armed services environment during the previous year. (UK Ministry of Defense, Feb. 2014.) Comparable statistics are not easily obtained for Canadian military personnel. The Auditor General of Canada did look at the issue in 2007 and, through staff interviews, found almost no complaints of bullying in the army and navy, but over three thousand in the Air Force. The AG report appears to have relied on a method involving formal complaints, which could result in considerable underreporting. It is known from sexual assault statistics, for example, that formal complaints dramatically underestimate actual occurrence of sexual assault. The same may be the case with formal complaints of bullying in military environments. A survey done in the Canadian Forces Atlantic Region provides a different picture for a small number of civilian employees working in a military setting. A survey method avoids the problem of underreporting from formal complaints.

Civilians in a Military Setting

A 2012 survey of morale was done at FCEA, a unit in the Atlantic region that employs a number of civilians,. The Unit Morale Survey included responses from 102 civilian employees of DND at FCEA. Stress levels were reported at moderate to high in approximately one third of this group, with several factors associated with high levels of stress. Among those factors were harassment, reported by 85%, and abuse of authority, reported by 82% of respondents. For 10 % of respondents, harassment caused either "a lot" or "extreme" concern" and for 15 %, Abuse of Authority caused "a lot" or "extreme concern". The findings represented a particularly large number of respondents who reported they had experienced or witnessed harassment or abuse of authority. Over half of the survey respondents expressed dissatisfaction with the military chain of command.

Police Services

RCMP

In November of 2011, the RCMP Public complaints commission investigated the question of bullying and harassment in Canada's national police force, releasing a report on the issue in 2013. There had been widespread reports from women Mounties of sexual harassment from male coworkers and supervisors in the Force earlier that year. In excess of 700 formal complaints had been filed between 2005 and 2011, representing about 2.5 percent of all RCMP members. Ninety percent of the complaints involved bullying. Sexual assault may have been underrepresented by the formal complaint statistics that were reviewed. The chair of the Commission for Public Complaints against the RCMP, Ian McPhail, told the media that the RCMP had an internal bullying problem and that it was overwhelmingly abuse of authority type bullying. Critics of the RCMP have expressed concerns that the senior management of the Force devotes more effort to discharging members who are off duty due to the impact of bullying on their health than any effort to actually address and correct the bullying problem in the Force.

Medicine

Medicine has a hierarchical structure that gives considerable power to senior physicians with regard to subordinates, especially medical students. There is some Canadian data on the rates of bullying and abuse of medical students Three University of Toronto Medical faculty members conducted an anonymous survey of fourth year medical students in 1992-1993. Their results showed some disturbing patterns. Twenty percent of their senior medical student sample had experienced a form of abuse that would constitute a legal offence, such as assault. In total, 8.3% experienced threats of bodily harm, assault or assault with a weapon and 13 %, mostly women, experienced unwanted sexual advances. The perpetrators were mostly clinicians, such as senior attending doctors, although the second largest group of perpetrators was nursing staff. The highest rate of abuse of medical students occurred in surgical settings. Students who had been abused showed a variety of trauma symptoms following the abuse. Among the students who had been physically abused, there was an increased risk that they would abuse students who were junior to them and also an increased risk that they would abuse patients. None of the students reported their abuse to the police, and only about a third reported their abuse to someone in authority in the medical school. They cited fear of reprisal as a reason for not reporting the abusive experiences[17].

Nursing

A variety of European studies show significant rates of bullying among nurses. For example, a survey of British nurses done in 2001

---

[17] Margittai, Moscarello, and Rossi, Bulletin American Academy of Psychiatry and Law, Vol. 24, No. 3, 1996

showed that 44 % of the nurses surveyed reported that they had experienced peer bullying in the past year[18]. A number of studies on bullying among nurses have described a particular form of bullying that is characteristic of women, relational bullying, where psychological methods, such as gossip or ostracism, are prevalent.

Studies on Canadian nurses produce high rates, comparable to the European statistics. According to data from Statistics Canada 2005, 50 % of Canadian nurses reported emotional abuse at work. There is evidence to suggest that bullying of entry-level nurses contributes to significant losses of new nurses to the profession, and that it is a contributing factor to widespread nurse shortages.

Teaching

Teachers appear to be subject to bullying from a range of sources. Aggression and hostility from students can be a problem if it is chronic or if the teacher has inadequate support and resources to address the problem. Similarly, teachers can be subject to bullying from parents, peers or school administrators. A study commissioned by three Teachers' Federations in Ontario confirms the point of view that teachers face multiple sources of bullying. Matsui and Lang Research conducted the survey for the Elementary Teachers' Federation of Ontario the Ontario English Catholic Teachers Federation of Ontario and the Ontario Secondary Teachers' Federation of Ontario in 2005. Approximately 1200 Teachers were surveyed in the study. Over one half of the teachers responding to their survey reported that they had been bullied personally during their professional careers. One in fifteen had been the target of physical violence while teaching. Aggressive behavior from students was most common with 36% of teachers reporting this form of bullying. The second most common was bullying by parents with 36 % of elementary school teachers reporting this problem. Bullying by administrators or colleagues produced less frequent formal complaints. However, teachers who reported bullying by administrators showed more stress symptoms and were more likely to have taken time off work.

---

[18]   Quine, Workplace Bullying in Nurses, Journal of Health Psychology 2001 6 (1)

All forms of bullying were associated with a range of stress symptoms and periods of stress leave from work.

Law

The culture of the legal profession values aggressiveness, which is associated with success and profitability in legal careers. Research on problems personality types, such as psychopathy,[19] indicates that the legal profession attracts a particularly high number of people with problem personalities, particularly those with deficits in empathy and conscience. These aspect of the profession suggest that there could be particular problems with bullying in the legal profession

According to the American Bar Association, bullying is a persistent problem in the legal profession, which provides "fertile ground for bullying behaviour"[20]. In support of this notion some survey findings show a problem in the profession. Lawyers' Weekly in Australia published a study which showed that half of the women lawyers and one third of the men surveyed reported that they had personally encountered bullying in their workplace [21].

In Canada, lawyer "incivility" came under increased scrutiny in the wake of the Grola case, which was heard before the Law Society of Upper Canada in 2012. The Law Society handed Grola a two-month suspension for his "uncivil" conduct during a hearing. The issue was discussed further in a 2012 issue of Canadian Lawyer, in an article by Lee Akazaki [22]. He described how the profession tolerates some antisocial behavior and incivility, especially by those who are successful, He asked lawyers to consider when the culture of aggression in the law crosses the line to become abuse. He expressed the view that the legal profession is in the process of changing its values to become more collaborative and that the change had reached the point that "smart no longer means antisocial" among lawyers.

---

[19] Kevin Dutton, The Great British Psychopathy Survey, 2013: Lawyers ranked #2
[20] American Bar Society, November 2014
[21] Bullying Rates Alarming, Lawyers' Weekly, Feb 4, 2014
[22] Lee Akazaki, Canadian Lawyer, 2012

It could be said that the legal community has a problem with bullying that is very different from the problem in the teaching profession. Teachers are subject to bullying from multiple sources, whereas lawyers appear to have multiple potential targets for their bullying behaviour: junior lawyers, female lawyers, minority lawyers, office staff and clients are all at risk from lawyers who are bullies.

Academia

There has been recent research on bullying in higher education, university and college settings. Loraleigh Keashly conducted a thorough review of the topic in her 2010 article Faculty Experiences of Bullying in Higher Education[23]. She examined 11 studies from Europe and North America and found that the rates of bullying in academic settings appear to be high in comparison to general population work settings. The average rates of bullying experienced by faculty surveyed ranged from 20 to 50%. There were some distinctive features of the bullying they reported. Faculty report that the majority of their bullies are colleagues. There were also higher rates of "mobbing" where two or more bullies had harassed a target colleague. The other very distinctive feature of the bullying reported by academics was the duration of the bullying: a large percentage of respondents who were bullied reported bullying that persisted for five or more years. The forms of bullying tended to focus on threats to professional status or reputation. Untenured faculty were at higher general risk for bullying. The tenure system may also be a significant factor in the duration of the bullying experienced by academics and the typically peer on peer nature of the bullying, which is distinctive to this work environment.

One Canadian study is that done by McKay et al, in a mid sized Canadian University in 2005[24]. The findings were consistent with those reviewed by Keashly from Europe and the US. Respondents reported that 52 % of the faculty who responded had experienced bullying and for 32 % of the faculty respondents, the bullying they

---

[23]   Keashly, Administrative Theory and Praxis Mar, 2010, Vol 32 (1) 48-70
[24]   McKay et al, Workplace Bullying in Academia: A Canadian Study. Employee Responsibilities and Rights Journal, June 2008, Vol 20 (2) 77-100

experienced was rated as "serious". New and untenured faculty were at particular risk. The costs of bullying in the university environment included faculty turnover and reduced engagement with work by bullied faculty.

Civil Servants

Canada's civil service is surveyed every three years and some of the resulting information gives a picture of rates of bullying experienced by public servants.

The 2011 survey results show that the rates of bullying reported by this group remain consistently high, with approximately 30 % of the employees in the public service sector reporting that they experienced harassment over the previous two years. The reported sources of bullying were in rank order: superiors, coworkers, the public, subordinates and people in other government departments. The highest rates of reported harassment was experienced by, in order, disabled at 50%, aboriginals at 42 %, women at 31 % and visible minorities at 31%. Government cutbacks were thought to be a contributing factor to the high rates of reported bullying. Bullying was associated with a wide range of problem outcomes in the workplace. There were high rates of psychological problems in bullied employees. The resulting disability claims associated with workplace bullying accounted for about one half of the workforce's disability claims. In spite of the high rate of reported bullying in the group, there were few formal complaints.

CHAPTER 5

Rate your own Bullying Experience

Bullying Checklist

Duration of the bullying

Less than a month	1
One to six months	2
Six months to a year	3
One to two year	4
Two to five years	5
Five years or more	6

Frequency of the bullying

Occasional, once a month or less	1
Weekly, most weeks	2
Daily most days	3
Daily more than one incident a day	4

Organizational Role of the bully

Subordinate	1
Peer	2
Supervisor	3

Senior management   4

CEO   5

Type of bullying behavior Check all types that apply to your situation

Unreasonable criticism
Unreasonable work demands
Being taken off valued work tasks
Yelling
Humiliation
Name calling
Physical intimidation
Sexual harassment
Nasty personal rumors
Creating a paper trail that can lead to dismissal
Direct threats to your work security, dismissal etc
Other

Number of types of Bullying Behaviour Listed Above

1-2   1

3-5   2

6-8   3

9 or more   4

Physical Health Effects
Number of new health problems since the bullying began

One or two mild problems   1

One or two moderately serious   2

One or more very serious health problems   3

Sleep Disorder

Mild   1

Moderate   2

Severe   3

Psychological Health Effects

Mild anxiety and or depression	1
Moderate anxiety and or depression	2
Significant anxiety or depression, With a need for medication	3
Symptoms make it difficult to cope at work	4
Symptoms make it necessary to take leave from work	5

How much of your time and energy is consumed by the bullying

Occasional demand on time and energy	1
Regular demand on time and energy	2
Constant demand on time and energy, bullying consumes attention and time	3

Personal and Family Circumstances
Social Support

Supportive family, partner/spouse and friends	1
Some social support	2
Poor social support	3

Financial position

Good Financial Position, eg assets, savings or spouse has a good job	1
Moderate Financial Position, eg your family needs your income, you have financial obligations, some debts	2
Difficult financial position, eg single parent with several debts	3
Poor financial position, eg the only source of Family income is your job, many debts	4

Available Professional Supports

Several good supports, GP therapist, union representative or other	1
One or two good professional supports	2
No professional supports	3
Professional supports are antagonistic	4

Threats to your reputation

Little threat to your reputation	1
Moderate threat	2
Very serious or damaging threats to your reputation	3

Threat to your career

Mild	1
Moderate	2
Severe	3

Difficulty in finding a new job

Some prospects for other jobs	1
Uncertain prospects for other jobs	2
Poor prospects for other jobs	3
Loss of current job would risk unemployment or loss of career	4

How to interpret your score

If your score is in the 1 to 17	Mild Bullying
If your score is in the 18 to 30	Moderate Bullying
If your score is in the 31 to 44	Serious Bullying
If your score falls at or above 45	Severe Bullying

Maximum score 54 points

CHAPTER 6

Survival Strategies for Coping with Workplace Bullying

Place the Blame Where it Belongs

Good psychological health requires that an individual deal with questions of blame in a balanced and realistic manner. Accepting too much or too little responsibility can both be problematic. People who have been subjected to some form of abuse, such as spousal abuse, will typically place too much blame on themselves. This is also likely for a person who has been subjected to abuse or bullying in their workplace. There can be instances in which a target has contributed in some manner to their abuse, for example, telling too much personal information to people at work or confronting a powerful person injudiciously. If a targeted individual has contributed to their abuse in some way, it is best to accept and learn from that experience. However, most of the time, people are targeted in the workplace for reasons that carry no blame. Someone may be targeted for being particularly good at their job, for standing up for the right thing, for speaking out about something in the public interest or for having some human vulnerability like cancer. Just as in cases of spousal abuse, the person with the real problem is the abuser and the responsibility belongs to the abuser; in this case, the workplace bully. To survive workplace bulling, it is vital to see the bully for who they are, someone with a significant problem, even though others may admire them and they may hold a high status in the organization.

One of the most serious and harmful consequences of workplace bullying is that it can rob the targeted person of their pride and sense of worth. At its worst, bullying invades the target's thinking and, in that way, it does its greatest damage. It is essential that any person enduring workplace bullying develop a clear and firm understanding of where responsibility belongs. That is the only way the targeted person can be protected from this severe and insidious consequence of workplace bullying.

Should You Confront the Bully?

Sometimes targets of workplace bullying are advised to personally confront the bully and tell them in clear terms that their bullying behavior is unacceptable. There may be some situations that such a confrontation would help to curb the bullying. However, those would generally be situations where the bully and target hold similar levels of power, or where the bully is a subordinate to the target. Whenever the bully holds some type of formal power over the target, confrontation would not be an advisable strategy. Confronting a power holding bully could cause an escalation of the bully's behavior to new levels of retaliation. Confrontation is not the only option for dealing with a bully. Clear and assertive communication is generally helpful in difficult workplace situations. It is also helpful to maintain a neutral tone as much as possible. Expressive individuals would do well to cultivate a "poker face". Some bullies will feed off any sense they get that the target is distressed by their behavior.

Find Reliable Support

Good social support can significantly reduce the impact of any stressful experience. Having a supportive partner, a caring minister, compassionate friends or other forms of social support can help a person cope with the experience of being bullied at work. Most people who experience ongoing bullying need to talk about what is happening to them. There are looking for validation and want to tell the details of the latest workplace developments. Telling a trusted person can serve as a reality check, for example, serving to confirm that the bullying is outside the norm of workplace problems and aggravations. If the bullying is intense and prolonged, the need to talk about it can become proportionately intense. Spouses will complain that the targeted person can think and talk about nothing else but their experience at work. The emotional stress and intensity can place a strain on the best of relationships and may be more than some spouses or friends can handle. Talking to other people at work can be a double-edged sword. Having sympathetic coworkers can be quite helpful, since others at work can know about the relevant events, issues and personalities. Coworkers who are eyewitnesses to the bullying and who are clear that the bully's behavior is inappropriate can provide uniquely valuable confirmation for the targeted person. However, even otherwise reasonable and aware coworkers may want to distance themselves from the target at some point to protect their own interests. Sometimes, targets have a supportive ally at work for a while, but the ally later changes their position and blames the target. This can be particularly hurtful for targets of bullying and can further compromise their already difficult position in the workplace. It can be quite difficult to read where some coworkers really stand. A work environment dominated by a bully often has an active informal information collection system. Even an apparently innocent coffee time conversation during which a target confides in a seemingly friendly coworker can result in information being conveyed to the bully that is then used to harm the target in some way.

Targets of bullying should be wary of opening up to coworkers and of assuming that work place observers will understand the injustice of the bullying.

One of the most valuable forms of support is professional assistance, for example from a psychologist with expertise in workplace bullying. A good professional person can help the target understand what is happening and help them to cope with and lessen the impact of the bullying. The services of a psychologist may be covered under private insurance held through the workplace or there may be professional counselors available under a workplace sponsored EAP program. It can help to have a team of professionals coordinating their efforts to assist the person who is being bullied. As there can be medical complications from the stress that bullying creates, the individual's physician should be informed of the bullying situation and be should also kept informed about the role other professionals are playing.

Find Other People Who Have Had Experiences of Workplace Bullying

Wherever you can find other people who have had to deal with workplace bullying, it can give affirmation and help in ways that other support people cannot so easily offer. Finding other people who can understand what you are going through helps you regain a sense of normalcy, particularly where they are good, competent people who you can tell did not deserve the bullying they experienced. It is also helpful to meet people who have found ways to survive and grow from their experiences. Be selective. Someone who is stuck in bitterness and injury cannot provide you with the support you need while you go through your own experience.

Keep Detailed Records of Bullying Events

Detailed recordings of bullying events are especially valuable. Bullying events can be complex, and the stress they generate can be very high. Often, it is all the target can do to survive the bullying and attempt to protect their job. However, the time and effort to create an accurate record is well worth the investment. Only by keeping detailed diary recordings can a target have an adequate and reliable record of the bullying events. Make note of any witnesses to key events and if they are supportive, include written records of their observations. Any additional documentation that can be collected by way of letters, minutes from meetings or other forms of recordings are valuable and can be integrated with diary recordings. The written record should be kept in a safe place, preferably not in the workplace, and it should not be shared with anyone other than legal or mental health professionals working on the case on behalf of the targeted person. Therapists and lawyers have clear obligations to protect the confidentiality of their communications with their clients.

Being able to provide them with good documentation makes their work more effective. Good records allow the targeted individual to recognize patterns of behavior and trends over time. A well-documented written record can, of course, be of great value for hearings or legal proceedings that arise from the bullying.

Protecting Your Health

It is the nature of bullying in workplace situations that surviving it can be an endurance marathon, with the targeted person attempting to resolve or improve their situation over the long run in the face of setbacks and multiple enduring difficulties. It is this long-term stress that can damage health, as there are few breaks for the bullied person and virtually no safe place or period of time in which they can recoup their resources and attend to their own health. In light of such chronic stress, efforts to protect health and remediate the stress build up can be quite valuable.

Chronic stress will have effects on several body systems and will lead to increased levels of stress-related bio-chemicals. Regular physical exercise helps the body to burn off excess stress bio-chemicals. An additional and particularly valuable means of controlling the effects of stress build up is a daily method of physiological relaxation. Forms of yoga, meditation or simple muscle relaxation exercises help to control or reduce the chronic level of accumulated stress. It is also likely that regular use of relaxation will benefit sleep security, which can also become badly affected by chronic high stress levels. A procedure that is easy to perform at home is best, to ensure regularity. Timing the relaxation process to be used before bedtime may optimize the sleep benefit. Daily use will ensure the most benefit from relaxation.

Eating patterns and nutritional support can be compromised as a result of bullying. Some effort is advisable to maintain adequate nutritional support. Ensuring at least one nutritious and healthy meal a day can increase endurance over the duration of the bullying experience. Seeking the advice of a dietician or personal physician could be helpful, as could the addition of vitamins. Generally it is advisable to curtail caffeine such as intake from coffee or cola drinks, as too much caffeine can produce serious anxiety symptoms that will make life more difficult for the targeted person.

Many people turn to substances of various kinds when they are under chronic stress. Periods of high stress are certainly not favorable for efforts to change smoking or drinking habits. However, the dangers from alcohol, in particular, during times of chronic stress are worth noting. Alcohol may be soothing in the short run but vigilance is warranted, as the long term costs can easily outweigh the short-term benefits. Alcohol overuse will further degrade sleep security and can create a host of problems over and above those associated with being bullied.

Alcohol abuse will certainly degrade the target's coping abilities at a time when they need all of their wits about them to survive what they are going through. When a target develops a drinking problem, it is apt to be used to discredit their claims of workplace mistreatment. Similar concerns apply to other substances such as marijuana or prescription medications. Periods of high stress can create substance abuse risk in people who would otherwise not be at much risk. Unfortunately, any substance that serves to take off the edge of stress can compromise functioning over the long run and create new problems.

Sleep problems are common in situations of severe stress. Most people will turn to some form of medication to obtain relief. However, the benefits from medication tend to be short lived. During chronic bullying it is most likely that the structure of sleep will become compromised. That is, the deep rest stage of sleep would tend to get destroyed or suppressed. Unfortunately the effort for a quick fix through medication will produce little improvement in this vital stage of sleep. The best approaches to managing sleep disorder rely on sleep management systems that draw on non-medication behavioral methods. An excellent resource for the sleep deprived individual is No More Sleepless Nights by Dr Peter Haure. He directed the Mayo Sleep Disorders Clinic for many years and his book allows the individual reading it to benefit from his many years of experience. Sleep disorder can become enduring but with the right methods, it usually responds well to non-medication behavior management. Taking the time to learn good sleep management methods will spare the targeted person some long-range complications that will tend to degrade their health and functioning over time.

Emotional Processing and Mental Clarity

I have chosen to put these two important topics together because of the relationship between them. In dealing with traumatic events or extremely stressful events, the affected person will need to do work of the heart and work of the mind. Doing effective work to resolve emotions is fundamental to being able to do well in the cognitive work of understanding and learning. The emotions that will most likely accumulate during a highly stressful experience, such as bullying, are sadness, anger and fear. If strong emotions are not dealt with effectively, they will build up and eventually come out in unwanted ways. Relying on emotional control and suppression of emotion is inadequate and will eventually cause problems. It will help if a person going through bullying is able to find safe and private ways to release their emotions. This kind of emotional processing needs free and uncensored expression. It should never be done at work or on a work related computer. It could involve private writing, talking with a therapist or having a trusted friend or loved who can listen to the distress with empathy. As pent up emotion is released in a safe and private way, thinking capacity will clear. Then understanding and learning can progress.

We all function with a personal structure of beliefs. Life experiences can challenge the beliefs that we value. It takes time to process complex experiences to work out a set of beliefs that represent our current reality and serve us well. At the extremes of problem thinking are found, on the one end, overly naïve beliefs and at the other end, trauma-based beliefs. For example, someone may believe that all people are good and that their own goodness will ensure them favorable treatment by others. If such a person encounters a truly harmful person in their work place and endures damage caused by that person, they will face a more difficult challenge than a person who has a more nuanced understanding of human nature. The naïve person might need to evolve their thinking to include some concepts of harmfulness. For example they might come to believe: *most people are good and will treat to me in a fair, reasonable way. Some people are potentially harmful; it can take time to decide on the character of an individual who has caused me problems. If I am dealing with a truly harmful person, I need to accept that and realize most people would find the task challenging. I can probably develop better understanding of problematic people and can probably develop better skills for dealing with such people when I have to deal with them.*

One particular belief system that many bullied people need to examine are beliefs about merit and how merit relates to success. Our culture upholds the belief that people advance or succeed primarily on the basis of personal merit. Many people hold beliefs such as *"Work hard and you will succeed"." If you are having problems at work, it is probably your own fault."*

Being bullied will certainly challenge these beliefs. People on the receiving end of bullying are often capable, dedicated workers and the bullies are often successful for reasons that have nothing to do with merit. We also like to believe that justice is available for us in our society and in our organizations. When that belief is challenged, there is an opportunity to develop a new understanding of justice. When a person can no longer believe that justice will be delivered by people in control of their organization, or by some type of judicial figure, they might be able to develop a different view of justice, as something that needs to be constructed through a struggle against the odds. There is an analogy I like to use about the struggle for justice.

The Recruiting Office

In 1915, a young man enters a recruiting office to enlist in the Great War. He tells the recruiting officer "I want to sign up because I have heard that our side is winning and the war will soon be over, I have heard that the enemy is stupid and weak and I want to be part of this great cause." The recruiting officer is a grizzled old veteran. He tells the young man, "What you have heard is not true. The enemy is intelligent and powerful, they outnumber us and we don't really know if anyone is winning. There is no guarantee that our side will win in the end. No one can tell when the war might end and whether anything good will be achieved by it. The only real choices you have are What side are you on? and How will you will fight?".

Some of the most challenging work that people have to do after extreme stresses is the work examining and modifying their beliefs. When working with a psychologist or other mental health professional, this work is called cognitive therapy. Working with an experienced therapist can be quite helpful in this regard.

Maintaining Hope and Control in your Life

During extreme life experiences, our ability to have hope and find control in our lives can be diminished or even lost for a time. Cognitive therapy can help to find hope and reasonable control. An illustration from research on Vietnam era military veterans might be useful. The research looked at how men reacted in life and death situations. For example, thirty men might have been involved in an enemy ambush. As the troop of soldiers headed down a hill toward a village, the ambush began. The men at the front were killed and the men at the back saw it happening. Under the circumstances, their weapons were of almost no use to save the lives of their comrades at the front of the line. Some men froze and other men took a form of action such as firing their weapon, even though firing it had very little chance of accomplishing anything. The men who tried to take some kind of action, on average, showed lower levels of PTSD, than the ones who did nothing.

For the person living through bullying, it is vital to find ways to maximize control. Even when living though a long-term crisis, it can help to maintain the attitude that you will be the decision maker on the things that affect you personally. It is mainly up to you whether you continue your fight or seek a new job. Of course, you will want to consult closely with a partner who is living through the experience with you and may be directly affected by the risk to income and security. Many loved ones will advise you to give up the battle for justice and just go get another job. For the person who is at the center of the experience, it is rarely that simple.

If being bullied has challenged your sense of worth and your sense of justice, you will probably need to make a good fight before you can let go, make some kind of peace with what has happened and turn your energies to creating a new path forward. Practical considerations can be at odds with psychological and emotional survival in this regard. If a person ends their fight for what is right too soon, it can come at a high personal cost. Ultimately, your career belongs to you and you need to be the decision maker. Similarly, if waging a war for your job is taking a toll on your health, by all means consult with your doctor and your therapist, if you have one. Only you can best decide if you are at your limit and need to take a leave of absence from work. Generally, for most people, taking a leave of absence for stress in a bullying situation is not an easy option and it can come with its own price. If your job security is at risk, it is usually better to continue to work, if that is at all possible

Many people who have been bullied by someone in power ultimately lose their jobs or find it necessary to quit their jobs. That said, there are definitely times when the toll is too great and it is simply too hard to continue. In those circumstances, you will need the best professional support system you can find. It can be difficult and stressful to have to deal with an insurance claim for disability. Having a physician, and psychologist or other support professionals who understand bullying can make quite a difference.

Dealing with HR, Unions and Lawyers

In the early stages of bullying, most people will turn to the resources within their organization. Many organizations have formal policies and human resource offices that are officially designated to deal with problems like harassment. While there are probably good internal resources that are helpful to individuals who are being bullied in some situations, all too often the internal options are disappointing or ineffective. It is much easier for an organization to have a written policy than it is to put such a policy into action in complex interpersonal situations. Human resource officers may operate with the interests of the organization placed above that of the individual employee who has been bullied. It is probably best to explore these options with an open mind and modest expectations. Often the solutions that are proposed are not very appropriate or effective. For example, if a powerful bully has been targeting an employee under his authority, it is not appropriate to treat the problem as a " dispute" between equals and to propose mediation between them. That option will make it look like the organization has responded to the problem while little actual good comes out of it. Mediation can be useful but unless there are two parties of approximately equal power status, it is unlikely to be helpful. Similarly, many organizations will opt for an educational approach when someone is identified as a bully. Sensitivity training would do little to address behavior that has its roots in the bully's personality, nor would it do anything to change the power the bully holds in the organization. There is some risk with ineffective interventions, that the bully will resent the efforts made by the targeted person to find redress and will then escalate his bullying efforts.

Another type of assistance is that which a union can offer. The effectiveness of union representatives and union counsel will depend on their awareness of bullying dynamics. Sometimes a person living through bullying will need to collaborate with union personnel in such a manner that the union personnel become more knowledgeable about bullying as they respond to the particulars of a case. It is best to never assume that a person in a designated role will be expert in this area, as that is not always the case. With union representation, it is possible that both the target and the bully are members of the same union. This would put the union in a conflict of interest position such that the target would need to have clarification of how the union will adequately represent them.

Some bullying situations may warrant the involvement of a lawyer, as for example in a situation where the individual is not represented by a union. Where a lawyer is needed, it would be important to find one who has a good understanding of the dynamics of bullying. Working with any representatives who do not adequately understand bullying is likely to add further stress to an individual who is already under excessive stress.

Dealing with Injustice

If you were bullied at work and tried for a long time to get your case heard in some forum that could give a fair decision, you were probably sustained by the hope that you would eventually find some justice. It can be crushing to have your struggle for justice ultimately end in defeat. There is no easy way to deal with such an outcome. The psychological task is the work of grieving, a long and arduous process. During grief work, the individual must first find ways to safely allow waves of sadness and anger to pass. The longer the struggle to find a fair hearing and the deeper the belief that someone would eventually render a fair judgment, the deeper the grief will be and the longer it will take to process it. There are no shortcuts to grief work. Trying to be positive and denying the emotions will only complicate and prolong the grieving process. While grief can be frightening and difficult to experience, there is great benefit from doing this work thoroughly. It can be especially helpful to find a good therapist if you have not already obtained one. Unresolved grief and anger can cloud a person long after painful events have ended. By grieving adequately the individual gains back their emotional health and finds more peace with their painful experiences.

The time for positive focus comes after enough grief and anger has been released and resolved. Only when enough emotional work has been accomplished will the person have the mental clarity to be able to see a way forward. After grief work has been done, the person can consider what they have learned and how they want to take power again in their life. Some people reconfigure their working life so that they can have more control over it, such as opening their own business, doing consulting work or developing a private practice. There is less risk of being bullied in a form of employment that you control. It is during this consolidation phase that people can begin to think in new terms about how they can address their own experience of bullying and how they can contribute to a public dialog about workplace bullying.

It can be a valuable contribution to the public discourse on workplace bullying for a survivor of such bullying to tell their own story. Media coverage and written accounts serve to increase public awareness. Some survivors of workplace bullying refuse to accept any settlement that binds them to silence about their own case for this very reason. The silencing of victims of all sorts of abuse only serves to protect the perpetrators of that abuse and hinders any adequate public recognition and response to the problem. There are other sorts of contributions that survivors of workplace bullying can make when they have adequate recovery. Lobbying of governments, working with professional groups and interest groups to add an informed voice can serve to educate the public and raise awareness. Of course for anyone who endured significant bullying it can take a lot to survive the experience. First you need to survive, but just surviving is not enough for many people. Many people will want to find a new way to fight the wrong, to take part in a broader public struggle to raise awareness and push for more effective means of response to such a major problem.

CHAPTER 7

Canadian Legislation on Workplace Bullying

To date, five Canadian provinces have passed occupational health and safety legislation that is specific to workplace bullying.

Quebec

Quebec was the first province to pass legislation in 2004 prohibiting "psychological harassment" in the workplace in the Act Respecting Labour Standards. Sections of that act dealing with bullying are incorporated in the Quebec Labour Code to protect unionized workers. The Labour Standards Tribunal has provided examples of bullying such as rude, degrading or offensive remarks, spreading rumors, ridicule, shouting abuse, belittling employees, ignoring them or making fun of their personal choices.

Under the Quebec legislation, options exist for different groups of employees. Unionized employees may file a grievance since the legislation reads protection against psychological harassment into all collective agreements regulated pursuant to Quebec labour law. Non-unionized employees may file complaints with the Labour Standards Commission, which is then required to investigate the complaint. If no settlement is reached between the parties, the complaint may be referred to the "Commission des relations du travail", similar to a Labour Board, for adjudication. Public service employees not governed by a collective agreement, including members and heads of agencies, file complaints with the Public Services Commission. There is a 90-day time limit for filing complaints. Remedies for violation of the provisions on psychological harassment include the following: ordering the employer to reinstate the employee; ordering the employer to pay the employee an indemnity up to a maximum equivalent to wages lost; ordering the employer to take reasonable action to put a stop to the harassment; ordering the employer to pay punitive and moral damages to the employee; ordering the employer to pay the employee an indemnity for loss of employment; ordering the employer to pay for the psychological support needed by the employee for a reasonable period of time as determined by the Commission; ordering the modification of the disciplinary record of the employee.

The legislation contemplates comprehensive and effective remedies. It is important to note, however, that in cases where the psychological harassment results in illness, the monetary remedies are more limited because the no-fault workers' compensation provisions for monetary compensation are brought into effect.

Saskatchewan

In 2007, the Government of Saskatchewan proclaimed legislation expanding the definition of harassment under *The Occupational Health and Safety Act, 1993.* The new definition of harassment includes language to address personal harassment in the workplace, such as abuse of power and bullying. The legislation also allows for the appointment of an independent adjudicator to hear appeals arising from harassment complaints. Implementation began with the creation of a new Harassment Prevention Unit within the Occupational Health and Safety Division of Saskatchewan Labour. The new unit was set up to focus on enforcing the anti-harassment legislation and educating workplaces on the new definitions and complaint process.

Ontario

In 2009, Ontario passed Bill 168, the Occupational Health and Safety Amendment Act; Violence and Harassment in the Workplace. The law addresses some worst case scenarios and specifies the responsibilities of the employers with defined consequences for non-compliance. "Workplace harassment" is defined in Bill 168 as "engaging in a course of vexatious comment or conduct against a worker in a workplace that is known or ought reasonably to be known to be unwelcome".

The act states that; An employer shall,

> prepare a policy with respect to workplace harassment; and review the policies as often as is necessary, but at least annually the policies shall be in written form and shall be posted at a conspicuous place in the workplace,
>
> an employer shall develop and maintain a program to implement the policy with respect to workplace harassment.
>
> an employer shall provide a worker with information and instruction that is appropriate for the worker with respect to workplace harassment
>
> include measures and procedures for workers to report incidents of workplace harassment to the employer or supervisor;
>
> set out how the employer will investigate and deal with incidents and complaints of workplace harassment;

The remedies available are those available under the OHS regulation. It would appear that in order for the harassment to be compensable that the employee would have to establish an illness or injury that resulted in the course of employment, and which would be covered by OHS as part of its usual mandate. The Ministry of Labour overseas OHS in Ontario.

Manitoba

Manitoba made changes to its Workplace Health and Safety Act, which came into effect in 2011. Those changes include protection from workplace bullying, which is termed "harassment". The Regulation only provides protection for employees in the conduct of their work in the workplace. The Regulation's definition states that objectionable conduct or comment has to be directed at a worker in the workplace. The legislation amends the definition of harassment with the following:

"harassment" means

> (a) objectionable conduct that creates a risk to the health of a worker; or (b) severe conduct that adversely affects a worker's psychological or physical well-being

Interpretation:

> 1.1.1(1) For the purpose of the definition "harassment" in section 1.1, conduct is
> (a) objectionable, if it is based on race, creed, religion, colour, sex, sexual orientation, gender-determined characteristics, marital status, family status, source of income, political belief, political association, political activity, disability, physical size or weight, age, nationality, ancestry or place of origin; or
> (b) severe, if it could reasonably cause a worker to be humiliated or intimidated and is repeated, or in the case of a single occurrence, has a lasting, harmful effect on a worker.

1.1.1(3) In this section and in the definition "harassment" in section 1.1, conduct includes a written or verbal comment, a physical act or gesture or a display, or any combination of them.

The definition here overlaps with the definition of discrimination (based on a personal characteristic) under human rights legislation. It is not clear what effect this will have with respect to choice of venue or remedies.

The legislation also speaks to the issue of management rights,

1.1.1(2) Reasonable conduct of an employer or supervisor in respect of the management and direction of workers or the workplace is not harassment. The Regulation requires all employers in Manitoba to: Develop and implement a written harassment prevention policy; and ensure that employees comply with the policy. The harassment prevention policy must: be developed in consultation with a workplace's safety & health committee or the safety & health representative or the employees — whichever applies; must include a specific definition of "harassment" that is spelled out in the Regulation and must include content statements and basic procedures for complaining. The Policy must be posted in a prominent location.

British Columbia

The British Columbia government passed amendments to *Bill 14, Workers Compensation Amendment Act*, 2011, which came into effect on July 1, 2012. The Minister of Labour had introduced the amendments in May, 2012, detailing changes to the *Workers Compensation Act* specifically designed to address the issue of workplace bullying.

The new amendments clarify that a worker is entitled to compensation for a "mental disorder", as opposed to mental stress, if that mental disorder is either: (i) a reaction to one or more traumatic events arising out of and in the course of the worker's employment, or (ii) predominantly caused by a significant work-related stressor, including bullying and harassment, or a cumulative series of such stressors, arising out of and in the course of the worker's employment.

The mental disorder must be diagnosed by a psychiatrist or psychologist as a mental or physical condition that is listed in the most recent American Psychiatric Association's Diagnostic and Statistical Manual of Mental Disorders at the time of the diagnosis. The Workers Compensation Board (the Board) may appoint a psychiatrist or psychologist to review such a diagnosis and the Board may consider that review in determining whether a worker is entitled to compensation for the mental disorder. Furthermore, in order to be eligible for compensation, the mental disorder cannot be caused by a decision of the worker's employer relating to the worker's employment, including a decision to change the work to be performed or working conditions, to discipline the worker, or to terminate the worker's employment.

These changes to the *Workers Compensation Act* apply to every decision of the Board or the Workers Compensation Appeal Tribunal on or after July 1, 2012, including decisions in respect of claims made but not finally adjudicated before July 1, 2012.

The amendments to B.C.'s *Workers Compensation Act* are a significant improvement in dealing with workplace bullying and are intended to provide a clearer, more straightforward method for targeting psychological harassment and bullying in B.C. workplaces. The long-term impact of these amendments will not be known for some time. The annual cost impact of these wage-loss claims is estimated at C$18- to C$20-million, excluding the administration costs of adjudicating claims or the anticipated increase in registered claims requiring adjudication. Additionally, it is unclear to what extent these amendments will impact the adjudication of matters by other tribunals such as the B.C. Human Rights Tribunal.

Federal Employees

In provinces with bullying legislation, there was an inequity due to the bifurcated jurisdictional structure in Canada. Only those employees working in provincially regulated workplaces benefited from the workplace bullying legal protections. Employees in federally regulated workplaces did not enjoy similar protection against psychological harassment. Since 2008 the legal protections against bullying have been covered under federal Occupational Health and Safety legislation.

Other Relevant Legislation

All jurisdictions except New Brunswick, Nunavut, Northwest Territories, and Yukon, have general legislation that can address workplace violence and/or harassment.

Where there is no legislation specifically addressing bullying, the general duty clause establishes the duty of employers to protect employees from risks at work. These risks can include harm from both physical and mental health aspects.

In addition, federal and provincial human right laws prohibit harassment related to race, national or ethnic origin, colour, religion, age, sex, marital status, family status, disability, pardoned conviction, or sexual orientation. In certain situations, these laws may apply to bullying.

Human rights tribunals also define and prohibit harassment, except that for a human rights case to be considered, it must be based on specific personal characteristics, such as gender, age, race, colour or religious beliefs. Thousands of harassment complaints are made each year to these tribunals with a far greater likelihood that they will succeed compared with a civil claim in court. This is because human rights tribunals are designed to interpret harassment and discrimination liberally. They exist to specifically adjudicate these very claims. Courtroom judges, on the other hand, often have little inclination to get involved in workplace interactions and order employees to behave reasonably.

CHAPTER 8

The Work that Remains to be Done

Public Education

One of the most impressive public education efforts of the 20th century was the one that exposed the health risks of smoking and made smoking socially unacceptable. Scientific and medical research came together with government and organizational initiatives to create a major shift in people's behavior and attitudes to produce great public benefit. It is an impressive achievement in the space of a few decades and represented the cumulative efforts of many individuals and organizations. The impact on public perceptions has been so significant that smoking has gone from fashionable to repugnant in the space of two generations. In a recent informal test of this attitudinal change, a group of teenaged girls were asked to look at two photos, one iconic photo of James Dean, in a white T shirt and one of Ricky from the Trailer Park Boys, both smoking cigarettes. The girls all quickly rated Ricky at the bottom of the attractiveness scale. Their reaction to the James Dean image was more interesting. They all looked at the image, and looked puzzled or conflicted over what they were seeing. Not one of them endorsed him as cool or good looking. Their comments were interesting. "He's in the middle", "He is mixed between good looking and not good looking." "He's kinda of cute but not really". It seemed to be the cigarette they could not process as part of an attractive man's image. It is an amazing change from how women fifty years ago would have reacted to that famous picture of James Dean.

Workplace bullying is not on the public radar or in its consciousness to any real extent. Most people trivialize workplace bullying and see it as relatively rare. The work that needs to be done in this regard is daunting. Education efforts regarding bullying to date have generally been devoted to bullying among school children. This kind of effort needs to be extended to workplace bullying to raise awareness of its prevalence, its cost to the public and the damage it does in individual lives.

People who have lived through the experience of being severely bullied in the workplace need to find ways of adding their voice to the efforts to raise public awareness. Personal stories are compelling in a way that statistics are not. This kind of contribution is best made when the individual has enough psychological recovery from their experience that they can articulate what they have learned and how the bullying has impacted their lives. There is no substitute for the personal stories in terms of the impact they can have on others.

Media Attention to Workplace Bullying

The media has a key role to play in the education effort. In Canada, the CBC has done some good radio programs on workplace bullying and Canadian newspapers have been covering the issue in feature articles from time to time. Major cases that come into the courts have a potential to galvanize public attention and they merit focused media attention. For example, the class action lawsuit being brought by women members of the RCMP is due to come into the courts in 2016. In March 2015, MacLeans ran a cover story feature on this issue and the legal case with personal stories. In the case of the women members of the RCMP, it took one or two dramatic personal stories breaking in the media for other women with similar experiences to band together, share their stories, organize and seek redress through the courts.

The history of boys abused at Mount Cashel is one that demonstrates the critical role of the media to create a public demand for accountability from the many government and church institutions that failed to address the scandal for more than a decade.

There had been rumors and occasional reports of abuse of boys by the Christian Brothers of Mount Cashel throughout the 60s and 70s. In 1979, The Royal Newfoundland Constabulary opened an investigation into abuse of the boys at Mount Cashel. The investigation was then stopped by the Chief of the RNC on orders of the Department of Justice. A second RNC investigation of Mt Cashel in 1982 resulted in only one Brother being charged and convicted. Then, in 1989, there were a series of media revelations starting with a caller to an open line radio program who referred to a cover up of abuse at Mount Cashel by the Newfoundland Government, the RNC and the Archdiocese of St John's. A Supreme Court Judge heard the program and the Crown Prosecutor's file on Mount Cashel was reopened. Around the same time, the Sunday Express, under the editorship of Michael Harris, began to publish explosive articles on the issue, detailing allegations that dated back to the 1950's. This media scrutiny resulted in such intense public reaction that there were calls for a public inquiry. In 1989, Premier Rideout of Newfoundland appointed Justice Samuel Hughes to head a Royal Commission of Inquiry. At the same time, there was a criminal investigation, which lasted until 1996. Over twenty members of Mount Cashel staff were charged and eventually nine were convicted. Approximately $27 million was paid in compensation to about 120 Mount Cashel victims of sexual and physical abuse. Several levels of the Roman Catholic Church attempted to protect their financial assets from the compensation claims of the victims, but the damage done to the Christian Brothers and the Catholic Church could not be undone. The Mount Cashel Orphanage was closed in 1990 and demolished in the mid nineties. Michael Harris' book <u>Unholy Orders</u> is the compelling story of Mount Cashel Orphanage.

Without the efforts of the media to expose the Mount Cashel abuse and call those responsible for it to account, the Mount Cashel story would have had a different ending. The media is vital to raising public awareness of workplace bullying.

Employer Education

There is a great deal of work to be done in the area of employer education when it comes to the topic of workplace bullying. Most companies and government agencies have some kind of formal written policies on harassment in place but they do very little to ensure any adequate response to the problem. Lip service from business and employers is not good enough for a problem of this magnitude The mechanisms to deal with bullying are poorly developed and biased toward protecting the interests of power holding bullies. Most organizations conduct their own investigations, which are inevitably compromised. There is a great need for well-qualified and genuinely independent forms of investigation of bullying in the workplace. For things to really change at the employer level, a major cultural change is needed. There was a time that physical abuse in the family was regarded as a private matter. Similarly, employers tend to regard instances of bullying as internal matters or disputes between individuals. Bullying is a form of abuse that should not be regarded as a private matter within a company. The typical interventions offered are inadequate or inappropriate. A broader range of interventions choices are needed. Sensitivity training and anger management training tend to be band-aid solutions that result in no real change in the bully. Mediation is inappropriate whenever there is a disparity between the bully and the target in their power holding status. Interventions that actively discourage bullying are greatly needed. For example, the incidence of bullying in an organization is apt to significantly reduce if persons with a clear track record of bullying suffer consequences, such as demotion or relocation to less desirable roles. Dismissal in egregious cases sends the right message to everyone involved, that bullying will not be tolerated, that the organization will uphold respectful and fair treatment of all its workers. It would be a good development for organizations to make more use of well qualified organizational psychologists who can bring a range of valuable assessment and intervention skills to assist organizations to respond more effectively to bullying.

Business leaders might pay more serious attention to the issue if the financial cost of bullying were to be emphasized. It might also be of some value if universities were to cover the topic of workplace bullying in course work for MBA, Human Resources, Public Administration and Hospital Administration. If individuals are educated on the issue in the course of their professional training they may go on to become leaders who can address the issue in the organizations they join after graduation. Public scrutiny is another aspect of promoting employer accountability on the issue. For public scrutiny to be effective, it would need to be based in some official policies such as more detailed government Health and Safety legislation at federal and provincial levels. For example, employers of a certain size could be required to conduct employee audits and provide the results to the relevant government department. Anonymous audits are likely to yield more realistic estimates of the prevalence of bullying in an organization. Another measure would be to require certain basic training in effective responses to bullying in all large companies in order for those companies to obtain certain types of certification or accreditation such as safety certification.

Lobbying for Legislative Changes

As noted in Chapter 7, only five Canadian provinces have legislation in place to deal with workplace bullying. For the other provinces, there will need to be a lobbying effort to convince provincial governments of the need for more effective legislation. People who have experienced workplace bullying can contribute to this effort by meeting with their Provincial MLA's and by organizing lobbying efforts to promote more adequate legislation in their own province.

Government Initiatives

The federal government has a key role in promoting adequate legislation to protect workers from workplace bullying. Lobbying efforts by individuals and organizations can be directed to individual members of parliament and to ministers of the federal government to promote improvements in legislation and more government initiatives to deal with workplace bullying. Workplace bullying is a widespread national problem with significant legal, human rights, health and safety implications. A variety of federal government departments such as Labour, Health, Industry and Justice have relevant mandates and the potential to become more involved in efforts to address workplace bullying. The federal government can institute a variety of measures and departmental structures to provide oversight to industry to protect the health and safety of workers.

Union Initiatives

Some unions are highlighting the issue of workplace bullying and are taking steps to respond to it. Unions have put on bullying workshops and have designated union personnel to specialize in this area of workers protection. The Nova Scotia Government Employees Union hosted a conference on workplace bullying in November 2014 with international experts. In 2015, the Canadian Union of Public Employees, presented a series of workshops for its members across Canada, titled Combating Workplace Bullying. A suitable goal for unions would be to have all of their union representatives reach a minimum standard of knowledge about workplace bullying and its consequences and for those union representatives to have expert resources available for their workers. For example, unions could identify investigators who are expert in the issue of workplace bullying and could exert pressure to have employers use the services of independent expert investigators. Collaboration among various unions would be valuable. Ongoing and coordinated efforts among diverse unions will serve to strengthen the ability of each of them to respond adequately to their members who have been bullied at work.

The Professions, Medicine, Law, Health Professions

At the most basic level, it would be good to see all the professions doing more to educate their members about workplace bulling. The topic could be covered through the course work that students take as part of their professional training.

Fraternal and regulatory bodies could collect data to determine if their members are being subjected to bullying during their working lives, particularly during the training phase. Regulatory bodies also have a role to play in their complaint adjudication process. Workplace bullying can and does ruin careers and results in the loss of valuable members for all the professions. Complaints about members of any profession bullying their subordinates or colleagues deserve serious scrutiny by regulatory bodies and warrant appropriate penalties.

The professions can promote research on the subject of bullying and interdisciplinary collaboration to develop means to overcome it in workplace settings such as hospitals or universities. One research topic is worth mentioning. We have some idea what types of individuals are targeted for bullying but not enough is known about the bullies themselves. Drawing a comparison to sexual abuse, it would never have been enough to determine what kind of individuals are targeted by sexual predators. Knowing the characteristics of the perpetrators of any form of abuse is essential. We certainly need to know more about who engages in bullying behavior in the workplace. Only good research that establishes the characteristics of workplace bullying can provide the foundation to develop appropriate interventions.

There are some goals that could best be addressed by particular professions. We need to develop better and more helpful interventions for the targets of bullying. That topic could involve response from Organizational Psychology, Human Resources, and Mental Health professionals. Another need is to develop better investigation and adjudication for workplace bullying. Investigators and adjudicators should have specialized knowledge, training and skills in the topic of workplace bullying to be able to render sound opinions and judgments. It could be quite helpful in this regard if a more diverse range of professional expertise were brought into investigation and adjudication of workplace bullying. For example, forensic psychologists have highly specialized skills that would be well suited to investigation and even to adjudication in this area.

CHAPTER 9

Valuable Resources

Websites on Workplace Bullying

Canadian Center for Occupational Health and Safety
http://www.ccohs.ca/oshanswers/psychosocial/bullying.html

The Workplace Bullying Institute
http:/www.workplacebullying.org/

Canadian Women's Health Network article on workplace bullying
http://www.osach.ca/products/resrcdoc/rvioe528.pdf

Canadian Bar Association Article on Workplace Bullying and Harassment in Addendum
http://www.cba.org/cba/newsletters/addendum01-08/news.aspx

Bullying in the Workplace 2009
Professional Institute of Public Service of Canada
http://www.pipsc.ca/portal/page/portal/website/slc/pdfs/bully.en.pdf

Red Cross Keep your work place healthy by eliminating workplace bullying
http://www.redcross.ca/what-we-do/violence,-bullying-and-abuse-prevention/in-the-workplace

UBC Bullying and Harassment Prevention
  http://bullyingandharassment.ubc.ca/

Crisis Prevention Institute Webinar on Workplace Bullying
  http://www.crisisprevention.com/Resources/Webinars/
  Workplace-Bullying-Define-Recognize-and-Respond

Minding the Workplace David Yamada
  https://newworkplace.wordpress.com/

Website of Glenn French, Workplace Assessments, Threat Assessments,
Investigations, Reports and Interventions for Workplace Bullying
  http://www.workplaceviolence.ca/

Self Help Website http://www.bullyonline.org/workbully/canada

Books on Workplace Bullying

Andrea Adams, with Neil Crawford, Bullying at Work: How to confront and overcome it (1992)

Paul Babiak & Robert D. Hare, Snakes in Suits: When Psychopaths Go to Work (2006)

Emily S. Bassman, Abuse in the Workplace: Management Remedies and Bottom Line Impact (1992)

Duncan Chappell & Vittorio Di Martino, Violence at Work (3rd ed., 2006) — Updated edition of an International Labour Organization report on workplace violence.

Noa Davenport, Ruth Distler Schwartz & Gail Pursell Elliott, Mobbing: Emotional Abuse in the American Workplace (2002)

Richard V. Denenberg & Mark Braverman, The Violence-Prone Workplace: A New Approach to Dealing with Hostile, Threatening, and Uncivil Behavior (1999)

Stale Einarsen, Helge Hoel, Dieter Zapf & Cary L. Cooper, eds., Bullying and Harassment in the Workplace: Developments in Theory, Research, and Practice (2nd ed., 2011)

Tim Field, Bully in Sight (1996)

Suzi Fox & Paul E. Spector, eds., Counterproductive Work Behavior: Investigations of Actors and Targets (2005)

Marie-France Hirogoyen, Stalking the Soul: Emotional Abuse and the Erosion of Identity (English ed., 2004)

Randy Hodson, Dignity at Work (2001)

Harvey Hornstein, Brutal Bosses and Their Prey: How to Identify and Overcome Abuse in the Workplace (1996)

Gary Namie & Ruth Namie, The Bully at Work: What You Can Do to Stop the Hurt and Reclaim Your Dignity on the Job (2nd ed., 2009)

Charlotte Rayner, Helge Hoel & Cary L. Cooper, Workplace Bullying: What we know, who is to blame, and what can we do? (2002)

Peter Schnall, Marnie Dobson & Ellen Rosskam, eds., Unhealthy Work: Causes, Consequences, Cures (2009)

Robert I. Sutton, The No Asshole Rule: Building a Civilized Workplace and Surviving One That Isn't (2007)

Kenneth Westhues, The Envy of Excellence: Administrative Mobbing of High Achieving Professors (2006)

Judith Wyatt & Chauncey Hare, Work Abuse: How to Recognize and Survive It (1997)

Books on Therapy and Recovery

Anxiety and Stress Management

David Clark, The Anxiety and Worry Workbook, 2011

Edna Foa, Reid Wilson, Stop Obsessing, 2001

Joseph Luciani, Self Coaching, The Powerful Program to Beat Anxiety and Depression, 2006

Richard O'Connor, Undoing Perpetual Stress, The Missing Connection between Depression Anxiety and 21st Century Illness, 2006

Robert Sapolsky, Why Zebras Don't Get Ulcers, An Updated Guide to Stress, Stress Related Diseases and Coping, 2004

Margaret Wehrenberg, The 10 Best Ever Anxiety Management Techniques, 2008

Mark Williams & Danny Penman, Mindfulness A Practical Guide to Finding Peace, 2011

Depression

David Burns, Feeling Good The New Mood Therapy, 2008

Paul Gilbert, Overcoming Depression, A Self Help Guide Using CBT Techniques, 2009

Dennis Greenberger, Christine Padesky, Mind Over Mood, 1995

Peter Levinsohn, Control Your Depression, 1992

Chris Williams, Overcoming Depression and Low Mood, A Five Areas Approach, 2015

Mark Williams and John Teasdale, The Mindfulness Way Through Depression, 2007

PTSD, treatment for PTSD

I Cant Get Over It A Handbook for Trauma Survivors Aphrodite Matsakis 1992 New Harbinger Publications

Ronnie Janoff-Bulman, Shattered Assumptions: Towards a New Psychology of Trauma (2002)

Sleep Disorder

No More Sleepless Nights Peter Haure and Shirley Linde 1991 John Wiley and Sons

How to Find a Psychologist

Alberta
The Psychologists Association of Alberta has a referral service
http://www.psychologistsassociation.ab.ca/

British Columbia
British Columbia Psychological Association has a Referral Service under the Find Help link
http://www.psychologistsassociation.ab.ca/

Manitoba
Psychological Association of Manitoba Has a Find A Psychologist link with Specialty listings
http://www.cpmb.ca/

New Brunswick
College of Psychologists of New Brunswick
Under Psychologist Link, site has a Finding a Psychologist link
http://www.cpnb.ca/

Newfoundland
Association of Psychologists of Newfoundland Labrador has a Find a Psychologist Link with Specialties
http://www.apnl.ca/

North West Territories
Association of Psychologists of the North West Territories
Contact Robert O'Rourke President psych@theedge.ca

Nova Scotia
Association of Psychologists of Nova Scotia
APNS Website has a Find a Psychologist Link by specialty
http://apns.ca/

Ontario
Ontario Psychological Association
Website had a Getting Help link, under About Psychology Link
http://www.psych.on.ca/

PEI
Psychological Association of PEI
Web site has a Private Practice Directory by Specialty
http://www.peipsychology.org/papei/

Quebec
Ordre des psychologues du Quebec
Web site has a Find a Professional Link
http://www.ordrepsy.qc.ca/en/

Saskatchewan
Psychological Association of Saskatchewan
http://www.ordrepsy.qc.ca/en/

Bullying Resource Sites, Support Groups and Blogs

Our Bully Pulpit: Canada Takes on Workplace Bullying

Articles, Resources, Videos and Stories about Workplace Bullying
http://bullyinworkplace.com/2010/03/13/canada-takes-on-workplace-bullies/

No Bully for Me
Anti Workplace Bullying Support Group in Vancouver, BC, Canada

Two targets of workplace bullies have set up a support group in the Greater Vancouver area (Canada) which meets monthly. Their aim is to share information pertaining to laws and regulations in British Columbia and raise enough awareness within the province to facilitate a change in attitude. They also offer mutual support, advice help and encouragement for fellow targets of workplace bullying. "To join or find out more, please email us at nobullyforme@gmail.com, letting us know how we may contact you, which city you are from and, if you like, a bit of background with regards to your bullying experience. We have a web site at http://www.nobullyforme.org/and a forum/board for people with updated articles and health info at http://p066.ezboard.com/bnobullyforme."

A Workplace Fairness Blog
David Yamata

David Yamata is a US lawyer who is an international expert on workplace bullying
His blog is informative, comprehensive and helpful
         http://www.todaysworkplace.org/tag/david-yamata/

Provincial Resources

Alberta

Alberta Learning Information Service
    Alberta's government site includes essential information and a list of services for professionals experiencing workplace bullying and harassment. According to the website, if the bullying is triggered by discrimination based on race, ethnicity, age, religion, disability, etc. you may be covered under the Alberta Human Rights Act. You may visit their site at www.albertahumanrights.ab.ca or call their toll-free number, 310-0000 and enter 780-427-7661 for north of Red Deer or 403-297-6571 for Red Deer south.

Alberta Government: Employers, What you need to Know about Bullying in the Workplace https://alis.alberta.ca/ep/eps/tips/tips.html?EK=11594

Government of Alberta
Bullies at Work
    https://alis.alberta.ca/ep/eps/tips/tips.html?EK=11608

Alberta Workplace Health and Safety Bulletin
Preventing Violence and Harassment at the Workplace.
    http://work.alberta.ca/documents/WHS-PUB-VAH001.pdf

British Columbia
British Columbia Ministry of Labour Employment Standards Branch
    The site offers a Self-Help Kit for employers and employees, who are unable to resolve disputes internally. Complaints such as bullying and harassment may go through the process of investigation, mediation and adjudication depending on the merits of the case and the parties involved.

    WorkSafeBC has developed policies and resources related to workplace bullying and harassment.

    BullyFreeBC www.BullyFreeBC.ca
    BullyFreeBC is a group of individuals and organizations mounting a campaign aimed at eliminating workplace bullying. The goal of the campaign is to create awareness about bullying in the workplace, provide links to resources dealing with bullying, and ultimately assist with the development and drafting of workplace anti-bullying legislation. BullyFreeBC has been an aggregator of content dealing with bullying. One of the major areas of emphasis has been on research with respect to the implementation of workplace anti-bullying legislation. A paper by Karolina Dec on the possibility of amending the BC Workers Compensation Act to include anti- bullying language is attached.

Manitoba

Manitoba Federation of Labour
    Brian Campbell, Psychological Harassment and Bullying in Manitoba Workplaces 2009

    Manitoba – Winnipeg Health Region Workplace Bullying is a Health Hazard The Winnipeg site contains helpful tips and information on how to stop and prevent bullying. Click the link for the Region's

Respectful Workplace Policy to see further resources including contact information of organizations that may help you. For more information, read our previous post about workplace bullying.

New Brunswick
The New Brunswick Advisory Council on the Status of Women issued a position statement on Workplace Bullying in March 2007

Toward a Respectful Workplace site at University of New Brunswick

Newfoundland
Government of Newfoundland

Maintaining a Harassment and Discrimination Free Workplace A Guide for Managers and Employees

Public Service Secretariat website for the Harassment and Discrimination-Free Workplace Policy or contact your Strategic Human Resource Management Unit for more information. www.exec.gov.nl.ca/exec/pss/working with_us/policies.html

Nova Scotia
Nova Scotia Government
Respectful Workplace Policy: Putting Bullies Out of Business
NS Department of Environment and Labour April 2007

A Workplace Violence Prevention Strategy for Nova Scotia
http://www.gov.ns.ca/lwd/healthandsafety/docs/Workplace
ViolencePreventionStrategy.pdf

Ontario
Ontario Ministry of Labour
Workplace Violence and Workplace Harassment
http://www.labour.gov.on.ca/english/hs/sawo/pubs/
fs_workplaceviolence.php

Ontario Ministry of Labour (MOL)

While the ministry prefers internal resolution of the complaint, the bullied or harassed employee may seek assistance of their nearest MOL office. Visit their site for the complete list of offices and contact information.

Ontario Safety Association for Community and Healthcare. Bullying in the Workplace: A Handbook
>   http://www.cwhn.ca/en/node/41612

Workplace Mental Health Promotion
Harassment Violence Bullying and Mobbing
>   http://wmhp.cmhaontario.ca/workplace-mental-health-core-concepts-issues/issues-in-the-workplace-that-affect-employee-mental-health/harassment-violence-bullying-and-mobbing

Justice at Work
Free legal advice to low and middle income Ontario workers
>   http://www.justiceatwork.ca/default.aspx

PEI
PEI Workplace Violence and Harassment Laws
>   http://www.wpvcorp.com/provincial-workplace-violence-harassment-safety-laws/prince-edward-island/

Quebec
>   Quebec Commission des normes du travail

The Commission des normes du travail offers a comprehensive information kit for French-speaking Canadians that would help them fight and prevent bullying.

Saskatchewan
WorkSafe Saskatchewan
Workplace Violence
>   http://www.worksafesask.ca/prevention/workplace-violence/

Unemployed Workers Help Center Saskatchewan
Employment Insurance Information and Advocacy
>   http://www.unemployedworkerscentre.org/

Lightning Source UK Ltd.
Milton Keynes UK
UKHW01f2206290818
328008UK00001B/101/P